INVESTING FOR Total Return

The Low-Risk, High-Return Approach to Investing for Income & Capital Appreciation

Peter D. Heerwagen

Probus Publishing Company
Chicago, Illinois

Library of Congress Cataloging in Publication Data Available

ISBN: 1-55738-005-8

Printed in the United States of America

1   2   3   4   5   6   7   8   9   0

DEDICATION

To my father
Herbert A. Heerwagen
who loves to promote my books.

Preface

The financial markets have become extremely volatile, more volatile than ever seen in our lifetimes. The Dow-Jones average drops 140 points in a single trading session, then jumps up 57 points one day in the following week. Such sharp gyrations create anxious moments for individual and institutitonal investors alike.

Is there a way to cope with this market madness? Yes, by taking the "total return" approach to investing. Certain types of securities are purchased for their upside potential and downside safety. The goal is to put the risk-reward odds back in the investor's favor.

I use the total return principles outlined in this book to manage my client's accounts. During the difficult second half of 1987, the accounts I managed outperformed the stock market by fifteen percentage points, as measured by the S&P 500 Index.

Investing for total return means seeking out those securities that provide higher than average current income as well as good prospects for capital appreciation. The former acts as a floor on the downside while the latter provides the chance for unlimited gains on the upside.

The total return investment philosophy can be used by any investor wishing to develop a different approach to asset management. It's particularly suitable for risk minimizers and capital preservationists who don't want to give up opportunities for capital gain. Recent changes in the income tax laws further enhance the bottom-line benefits of total return investing.

I started writing this book prior to the historic October 19, 1987 stock market crash. Little did I know how quickly total return investing would become such an important strategy for coping with the new investment climate.

Peter D. Heerwagen

v

Contents

Chapter 1

Introduction

Today's increasingly volatile financial markets require a different approach to securities investing. When the Dow drops by a record 508 points, or 22% in one day, as it did on Black Monday, October 19, 1987, and you suffer large losses, it's time to reassess your investment strategies. Preservation of capital must take on a new importance.

The purpose of this book is to inform readers about the benefits from a little-known but proven technique—total return investing—and to show them how to profitably implement it. The total return concept is basic to everyone's goal of reducing investment risk while increasing the potential for profit. It is a defensive strategy based on the premise that the best offense is a good defense. Its designed to put the odds for winning the investment game in the investor's favor. And recent changes in the tax law make total return investing more attractive than ever before.

It should be understood that the total return approach isn't a new fad. Successful investors have been applying it for years. In fact, two mutual funds specializing in total return investing have had excellent track records. Because they're prime examples of how to make this strategy work, a brief review of their investment philosophies and records is worthwhile.

The older fund, known as the Evergreen Total Return Fund, is run by the Saxon Woods Asset Management Corporation in Harrison, New York. Its five-year compound growth record through 1986 is an impressive 22.1% a year. It's been in the top group of growth-income funds for four of those five years and in the highest 6% of all equity no-load funds during that time span, according to *The No-Load Fund Investor*. And the fund managers haven't taken large risks to achieve these excellent results.

The Evergreen Total Return's objective, as stated in its prospectus, is "to achieve a return consisting of current income and capital appreciation in the value of its shares." The prospectus goes on to say that the emphasis on each component will be relatively equal, although changes in market conditions and interest rates will cause the fund to vary the emphasis in search for the optimum return for its shareholders.

The Evergreen Fund's strategy is to invest in common stocks and convertible securities with a good current rate of return, a potential for dividend increases, and an opportunity for capital growth. In addition, the fund deploys a defensive strategy to protect capital through yield support. This is a description of total return investing at its best.

A large portion of Evergreen's assets is invested in relatively high-yielding, conservative securities such as the common stocks of natural gas pipelines, electric utilities, and telephone companies, and convertible preferred stocks and convertible bonds issued by companies in a variety of industries. These are hard-core total return securities.

The other well-known total return fund is the Strong Total Return Fund, managed by Strong/Corneliuson Capital Management, Inc. of Milwaukee, Wisconsin. According to the prospectus, its objective is "to realize a combination of income and capital appreciation which will result in the highest total return while assuming reasonable risks."

The Strong Total Return Fund is a market-timing mutual fund. It switches assets from the stock market to the bond market to money market funds and back again, depending on the outlook for each of these markets. This is a flexible investment approach. Strong's managers look for the best relative values. In selecting common stocks, the emphasis is on determining asset-related value compared to market price.

The Strong Total Return Fund has also had an enviable record. Since its inception in 1982, the fund has averaged 26% a year compound growth rate through the end of 1986. This places it in the top 3% of all 500 mutual funds evaluated by Lipper Analytical Services. The Strong Total Return Fund has consistently beaten its stated objective of realizing a rate of return at least 5% greater than inflation.

You can aim for results similar to those achieved by Evergreen and Strong by applying the total return strategies developed in this book. In fact, you should be able to surpass their outstanding achievements because your investing abilities won't be constrained by such problems as large portfolio size, uneven flows of funds, liquidity needs, and slow-moving investment committees that many fund managers must contend with. And there's an added bonus. Thanks to the new tax laws, total return investors get to keep more of what they earn.

The Concept Explained

Exactly what is meant by total return investing? The concept relates to deriving both current income and future capital appreciation benefits from an investment. The returns from each component, when added together on an annualized basis, produce what is known as "total return" to the investor. The income portion is just as important as the appreciation potential in the total return philosophy.

The total return concept is probably most familiar to followers of the mutual fund industry. Many funds advertise their latest total return figures in the financial pages of major metropolitan newspapers and in the popular money and finance magazines. The funds simply sum up their net investment income dividends and appreciation in net asset value to arrive at the total return figure for a particular time frame. If the numbers look good, they'll advertise them. During periods of declining interest rates, even conservative bond funds will generate relatively high total returns; you'll see the fund management companies advertise them as well.

What are total return securities? Generally speaking, they're higher-yielding securities which have a good chance for capital appreciation. The appreciation is derived from growth in corporate earnings or dividends, a more positive outlook for the industry, the perception of a financially-stronger company, or a combination of these factors. Such bullish developments translate into higher security prices.

The classic total return security is the convertible bond. It provides a reasonably high current return from interest payments plus the possibility of capital appreciation if the price of the common stock into which it is convertible increases. On the other hand, because of its defensive characterisitics, it provides downside protection during stock market declines. Convertible securities are fully discussed in Chapter 6 of this book.

A Conservative Investment Approach

The total return investment philosophy is more conservative than other strategies followed by many investors. Preservation of capital is a cornerstone of its application within the investment spectrum. It is not a get-rich-quick scheme. Don't expect to hit home runs with total return investments, although from time to time this joyous event may happen.

Instead of investing in the more glamorous, pure growth situations favored by many investors, the total return advocate gives up some growth potential for the assurance of current income. The latter is more certain, whereas no one can guarantee that the capital appreciation component of the total return equation will ever be realized.

Furthermore, higher-yielding securities are usually less volatile because the yield acts as a floor on their price. In the bloodbath of October, 1987, when the Standard & Poor's 500 Stock Index fell 15% in a few days, utility stocks dropped by only 5.4%, telephones by 7.6% and international oils by 8.2%. These groups of stocks all provide higher than market yields.

The Total Return Philosophy Applied

One of the most successful money managers is John Neff of the Vanguard Group of mutual funds. He manages the famous Windsor Fund, among others. Because his mutual funds have exceptional track records in both up and down markets, his investment philosophy merits attention.

Neff feels that stocks with good dividend yields don't necessarily have limited appreciation potential. He's a contrarian investor who seeks low price-earnings ratio stocks with high yields. But he'll also buy stocks with low yields if they have unusually high growth prospects due to robust dividend increases. When these growth stocks have a nice price run, he sells them and buys other high-yielders. John Neff is the classic total return investor, and a very successful one.

The total return investment strategy is not limited to the purchase of common stocks. Corporate bonds, preferred stocks, limited partnerships, and even option writing can be used to achieve total return goals. Each is analyzed in later chapters of this book. The recommended portfolio mix of total return securities will vary according to the investor's needs and preferences.

On the other hand, securities that don't offer solid prospects for total returns are not discussed in this book. They include money market funds, tax-exempt bonds, pure growth stocks that pay no dividends, high-rated fixed-income securities, and hard assets. This last category covers assets that don't generate any current income, such as gold, silver, collectibles, and raw land.

Impact of Tax Reform

Before passage of the Tax Reform Act of 1986, many individual investors had good reason to chose a growth stock investment strategy over a total return strategy—favorable tax treatment for capital gain-derived income. Prior to 1987, a 60% exclusion of capital gain income was allowed, with the balance taxed at regular rates. Therefore, taxpayers in the 50% bracket paid only a 20% tax on capital gains from security sales.

Meanwhile, ordinary income such as interest and dividend payments was 100% taxed. The 50% bracket investor paid fifty cents in taxes on every dollar of ordinary income. *Because of this, high tax bracket shareholders opted to invest for capital gain income to raise their after-tax returns.* Table 1 shows the impact of the Tax Reform Act on the maximum individual and corporate tax rates.

Table 1: Tax Rate Changes after Reform

| | Before Reform | | After Reform |
	Ordinary Income	Capital Gain Income	All Income
Individuals	50%	20%	28%[*]
Corporations	46	28	34

[*]33% for single and married persons with taxable income between $43,150–$89,560, and between $71,900–$149,250, respectively; then dropping to 28% again. These amounts will be adjusted for inflation beginning in 1989.

The net result from tax reform is that ordinary income will no longer cost more in taxes than capital gain income. All income is taxed at 28% (33% for high earners) regardless of source. The total return investment strategy has clearly become more attractive with its emphasis on the greater certainty of the receipt of current income versus capital gain income.

Consider the following example (Table 2) of a current income-oriented investment and a growth investment, both of which are expected to generate a 12% total return. The return on the former was comprised of 8% current income and 4% capital appreciation, while all the return on the growth investment was from appreciation. Assume that the investor was in the highest possible tax brackets of 50% before tax reform and 33% after reform.

Table 2: Comparison of Returns from Income and Growth Investments

| | Before-Tax Returns | | After-Tax Returns | |
	Current Return	Capital Apprec.	Before Reform	After Reform
Income Investment	8.0%	4.0%	7.0%	8.0%
Growth Investment	–	12.0	9.6	8.0

As can be seen, the "before tax reform" advantage was clearly with the growth investment, which had a 9.6% return compared with a 7% return for the income investment. The after-tax return on the income investment increases from 7.0% to 8.0% under tax reform, while the return for the growth investment declines from 9.6% to 8.0%. Both returns are now equal. The only difference is that you can defer taxes on capital appreciation as long as you don't sell the security, whereas with current income, you pay taxes as it is received. But this advantage is slight except in the case of long-term holds of five to ten years or more.

The Tax Reform Act of 1986 will probably bring another plus to total return investors. Before tax reform, many corporations retained a large portion of earnings to plow back into the business. If they could earn more on these additional company assets than shareholders could on any after-tax dividend income, then rising corporate earnings could, in effect, be transformed into capital gain. This assumes the capitalization rate (price-earnings ratio, or the price investors are willing to pay for each dollar of earnings) stayed the same. As indicated earlier, with the 60% exclusion, capital gain income was markedly better than dividend income for most investors. It was taxed at a maximum rate of 20% rather than 50%.

Tax reform has created several incentives for public companies to raise dividends, thus making their shares more attractive to total return investors. Corporate tax rates have dropped from 46% to 34% (see chart above), giving companies greater after-tax cash flow. Individual tax rates are lower, which means dividend income is more valuable to shareholders on an after-tax basis. Finally, the previously mentioned loss of the capital gains deduction makes reaching for capital gains a less attractive propositon for stockholders. Clearly, there's less incentive to take on more risk if the tax rates are the same for both types of income.

Benefits of Total Return Investing

What are the benefits from total return investing? First comes exposure to less risk than through investing in either pure growth or pure current income situations. Total return investing is almost synonymous with capital preservation. Growth investors are much more subject to the ups and downs of the stock market and corporate earnings. Fixed-income investors are at the mercy of interest rate movements.

Total return investors, on the other hand, are blessed with the best of both worlds. They receive high current income to offset losses from stock market drops. With respect to the particular type of bonds total return investors purchase, the issuing company's cash flows and credit quality are on the upswing. This acts to lessen drops in the price of its bonds due to a rise in the level of interest rates.

The fact that a company can consistently raise its dividend helps provide a cushion for the stock during weak markets. The dividend creates a floor against further price deterioration. If the dividend is increased in a falling market, the chances are more investors will eventually be attracted to the stock because of its sound fundamentals. There's no better defense in a declining market than a growing stream of income.

In the 1974-75 period, when the stock market suffered one of its worst beatings, Exxon Corporation paid a high dividend on its common—$2.80 a share. The stock fell along with all stocks during this terrible bear market. But when it reached $28 a share, the fall stopped, for at that point the Exxon common share yield was a hefty 10%. This attracted astute investors who realized the dividend appeared secure based on excellent cash flows. As a matter of fact, Exxon boosted the dividend in the following year.

A second benefit of total return investing is that with less risk comes lower portfolio volatility. The stock prices of dividend paying companies are fairly stable, whereas those of growth companies have more pronounced percentage movements up and down. Convertible securities are even less volatile than common stocks. And most limited partnership interests aren't even traded. Therefore, the aggregate value of a total return portfolio shouldn't fluctuate as much as other portfolios. This makes for easier sleeping at nights and less worry during the day.

Common stocks in the total return portfolio will characteristicaly have lower betas—an indicator of how a stock moves in relation to the whole market—than those in a growth portfolio. (Betas aren't calculated for bonds.) A beta of 1.5 indicates a rise and fall of 15% for every 10% change in the stock market; a beta of .80 indicates an 8% movement up and down. The former is characteristic of a more volatile growth stock and the latter of a more conservative total return security.

A third benefit of total return investing is that because its proponents hold securities for the long-term, they tend to do less trading than other investors. This reduces transaction costs associated with buying and selling securities. It also defers income taxes on capital gain because taxes are not paid until gains are realized. Naturally, some events cause higher trading activity such as early achievement of appreciation objectives or a rapid deterioration in a company's finances, but these will be the exception rather than the rule.

The reason for lower trading activity with total return investing is that the fruits of this endeaver usually don't ripen until a reasonable period of time has elapsed. Profits go to the patient investor. As explained earlier, total returns are achieved through a combination of current income and capital appreciation. The latter is derived from higher earnings, dividends, and cash flow or an improved outlook for the company's prospects—these take time to develop, often several years or more. As the old Wall Street saying goes, "Slow and steady usually wins the investment race."

It appears that investors are willing to pay more for the certainty of current income over the insecurity of capital appreciation. It's more valuable. Witness the price action of the publicly-traded "dual" funds—closed-end investment companies that own a portfolio of common stocks. The dual funds have two classes of owners; income shareholders who are entitled to all the income from the portfolio, and growth shareholders who receive all capital appreciation when the fund is liquidated.

Interestingly, the income shares of dual funds sell at premuims to net asset values (NAV), while the growth shares sell at discounts to NAVs. This phenomenon is true for all six funds. The public clearly values current income more highly than potential capital gain. Fortunately, total return investors can get these same income benefits without paying any premiums.

Beneficiaries of the Total Return Approach

Total return investors fall into several categories depending on the special circumstances of each one. The first group includes those who want to minimize risk—that's just about everyone who has ever invested, young and old alike. Yet at the same time, these persons don't want to lessen their chances for achieving high investment returns.

The total return investor reduces risk by the type of security he buys for his portfolio. As indicated previously, higher-yielding stocks are less risky than pure growth securities because the yield helps support the stock price. Likewise, convertible securities have less downside movement than their underlying common stocks. Both high-yield stocks and converts offer the possibiity for capital appreciation.

A second group—owners of small pension plans such as IRAs, Keoghs, and SEPs—are prime prospects for total return investing. Most anyone involved with investing his retirement funds has to take a relatively conservative approach. Capital preservation is a must. This is particularly true if the person has to depend on these pension funds as a source of income in retirement.

Because investment earnings build-up in these retirement accounts on a tax-deferred basis (that is, they aren't taxed until withdrawn), there's no distinction between current income and capital gain income. The quicker that current income is added to the pension portfolio, the faster the reinvested earnings compound in the tax-deferred environment. With its emphasis on income, the total return strategy is a natural for small pension plans.

Retired persons form a third group of investors who will also find the total return strategy a good one to follow. The biggest fear retired persons have is running out of funds because inflation has eroded their capital base. To stay ahead, senior citizens must keep part of their portfolio in assets that grow, either in dividend-earning power or through capital appreciation, or preferably from both.

A portfolio invested 100% in fixed-income securities will gradually lose ground as inflation eats at the purchasing power of the interest earned, as well as the principal. If the cost of living increases at a modest 5% a year, in fifteen years a fixed $25,000 income will only be worth a little over $12,000. A total return philosophy can help in this regard because the retiree invests in securities that produce a growing stream of current income, and hopefully some capital appreciation, to offset the effects of inflation.

The next chapter will explain how to predict total returns and assess risks that you, the total return investor, will face when making investment decisions.

Chapter 2

Predicting Returns
and Assessing Risk

A s a total return investor, you must be able to predict total returns from each security considered for possible inclusion in your portfolio. This will enable you to compare the benefits of one security against another. Likewise, the total return investor must assess the risks associated with every security under consideration. You'll want to select those investments that promise the highest returns with a minimum amount of risk—those that have the best risk-reward ratios. This is the key to successful total return investing.

As you might guess, predicting returns and assessing risk are not easy tasks, even for professional investors; they're more an art than a science. But this should not sway you from going through the risk-return evaluation exercise. As you gain from experience, your judgment and intuition will improve to the point where the exercise will become second nature to you.

Predicting Total Returns

The total return investor must know how to calculate a stream of future total returns for a security. Because they're made up of two components, current income and capital appreciation, each part must be computed separately and then added together for every year you expect to hold the security.

In order to calculate the first year's income component, use the current security price and divide that into the annualized payment—either interest, dividends, or any other type of income distribution. This gives the current yield. Next project what you believe the expected price will be in one year. Subtract the current security price from it and divide the resulting number by the current price. This gives the percentage for the capital appreciation component. Adding the current yield and capital appreciation together gives the total annual return.

For the second year, the process starts over again using that year's beginning price as the base to calculate both the current yield and the expected appreciation. (Don't go back to the original price when calculating yields and future appreciation.) Projections for years out are done the same way, starting with the latest year as the base year.

The formula below shows how expected returns are calculated for a stock selling at $10 and paying $.50 in dividends for a 5% current yield. It assumes the dividend grows at 5% a year and the share price increases at the same rate. The total return is expected to be 10% for each of the three years.

Formula for Calculating a Stock's Expected Total Returns

Year D/P   = Y   EP - BP/BP   = CA Y + CA = Total Return

1 $.500/10.00 = .05 \quad \dfrac{10.50 - 10.00}{10.00} \quad = .05 \quad .05 + .05 \ = .10 \ = 10\%$

2 $.513/10.50 = .05 \quad \dfrac{11.03 - 10.50}{10.50} \quad = .05 \quad .05 + .05 \ = .10 \ = 10\%$

3 $.538/11.03 = .05 \quad \dfrac{11.58 - 11.03}{11.03} \quad = .05 \quad .05 + .05 \ = .10 \ = 10\%$

D - Annual dividend	EP - Expected price
P - Price	BP - Base price
Y - Yield	CA - Capital appreciation

With no growth in dividend or share price, the total return would be limited to just 5% because the stock would stay at $10 a share and the dividend would remain constant at $.50. All of the total return would emanate from the current income component.

Total returns can be predicted without considering income taxes, for under tax reform they have the same impact on both the current income and capital appreciation components. But you should always remember that total return projections are before-tax figures; after-tax returns will vary according to your individual tax bracket. Regarding pension funds such as IRAs and Keoghs, no taxes are paid until funds are withdrawn.

The typical growth security produces lower current yields but has higher capital gain potential. Growth companies plow back earnings into their operations to produce higher profits, rather than pay out a large portion to shareholders as dividends. Investors bid up prices now in anticipation of higher dividends later. Higher prices translate into lower current yields.

In analyzing a steady growth investment, annual appreciation can best be predicted by extrapolating historical data and making adjustments when necessary. Rather than doing detailed calculations, put ballpark figures together. Table 1 shows the returns from a hypothetical growth security over a five-year period.

Table 1: Total Returns for a Growth Security

Year	Current Income	Capital Appreciation	Total Return
1	3%	9.0%	12.0%
2	3	9.0	12.0
3	3	9.0	12.0
4	3	9.0	12.0
5	3	9.0	12.0

The projections for the growth security are 3% in current yield and 9.0% annual capital appreciation. It's assumed the dividend also goes up 9.0% each year to provide the stable 3% yield. (Remember, each year's yield is based that year's dividend divided by the beginning year's price.) Total annual returns are 12%. They must be compared with other returns available in the market place, along with the risk level of each. For example, if the projected return is at least 5% higher than yields available from a relatively risk-free investment such as a short-term government bond, then it may appear to be a good investment.

Predicting total returns for a turnaround security is a much more difficult task. It's hard to know exactly when the business recovery will occur, when the financial markets believe it has started, and when the price of the company's securities will respond favorably to its improved business prospects. Table 2 sets forth the expected total returns for a typical turnaround investment situation—a high-yielder with a depressed price due to its out-of-favor status with Wall Street.

Table 2: Total Returns for a Turnaround Security

Year	Current Income	Capital Appreciation	Total Return
1	7%	0%	7%
2	7	15	22%
3	5	25	30%

In this scenario, you assume it will take at least a year before a business comeback is on the way; therefore, no capital appreciation is likely to occur in the first year. In the second and third years the price of the security moves up smartly as the corporate financial news gets better. This produces capital appreciation of 15% and 25%, respectively.

It should be noted that by the third year the current income component of the total return equation drops from 7% to 5% because the dividend wasn't raised. Turnaround companies often use excess cash to pay down loans, upgrade facilities, build working capital, or expand capacity. Yet the third year's 30% total return is the highest of any year thanks to the 25% capital appreciation. This hypothetical investment is one that all total return investors would be proud to own.

Investing in the stocks or bonds of a fallen angel or financially-weak company may require taking on higher risks. But as the example above indicates, the projected rewards should also be higher. Remember, you should always be justly compensated for the risks you're willing to take.

The previous discussion focused on predicting total returns. This is not the same as realizing total returns, which happens when the security is finally sold for one reason or another. You should be aware that very rarely will realized returns match up exactly with expected returns. Usually your projections will be too optimistic, so temper them to what you believe is a realistic scenario. Try not to listen to Wall Street. Securities analysts are an eternally bullish group. Stockbrokers need to sell shares to earn commissions.

Generally speaking, the greater the level of risk and the higher the potential returns from an investment, the larger the spread between expected and actual returns. And the longer the projections go out in time, the more magnified these differences become. Therefore, total return estimates need to be constantly reviewed and revised based on new information as it becomes available.

Controlling Total Return Investment Risks

Just as total return investors must estimate returns, they must also be aware of investment risks, especially with today's volatile markets. The total return approach to handling risk can insulate you from near disaster in market routs. One of the keys to building capital is preserving it during market downturns. In fact, this can be more important than outperforming the market when it's moving upwards.

Total return investors believe that above-average investment performance can be achieved only through judicious control of risk. Although most investors would say that risk and reward are direcly related, total return disciples try to beat the odds by investing in securities with the most favorable risk/reward ratios. Risk reduction equates to preservation of capital, an important goal of the total return investor.

The bywords of the total return investor are "upside potential with downside safety." And in most cases the downside safety comes from the current yield support provided by total return securities. If total return investors were to graph their risk-reward ratios and compare them to those of aggressive and conservative investors, the graph line would fall in between the other two. It would look something like Figure 1.

Total return investors actually try to find appropriate securities that move their risk-reward lines to the right, as illustrated in Figure 2.

The rightward shift of the risk/reward line means that the total return investor achieves greater returns for the same degree of risk taken. When this is successfully done, it accomplishes the goal of making the investment odds more favorable to the investor—a truly powerful concept for profitable investing.

Figure 1: Risk-Reward Levels for Several Types of Investors

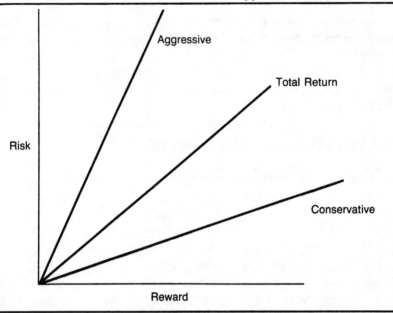

Figure 2: Total Return Risk-Reward Line Shifting to Right

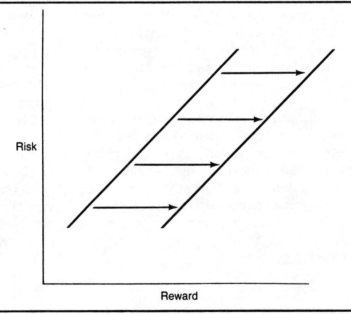

A thorough knowledge and understanding of the relationship of risk to reward is basic to any investment strategy. For total return investors, the most worrisome risks are market risk, business risk, and interest rate risk.

They differ in varying degrees depending on the type of security under consideration.

Market risk relates to fluctuations in the stock market, as measured by the popular averages, namely the Dow-Jones Industrial Average, the S&P 500 Index, or the NYSE Index. For total return investors, as with all equity investors, market risk is an important risk to consider. The prices of just about all securities are related to stock market movements. With total return securities, however, market risk is reduced because higher yields provide a cushion against downward price movements. Also, bond prices do not usually fluctuate as much as stock prices. Fixed-income securities that total return investors purchase should not have as much risk.

Business risk relates to the chances that a company which has issued securities experiences a business downturn or even fails. The investor is unable to anticipate the events peculiar to a company which will cause the value of its securities to decline. This risk is present with every security no matter what investment strategy is employed. It can affect the prices of bonds as well as stocks.

Total return investors try to reduce business risk through proper diversification, but this can never be entirely eliminated. They can also control this risk as it impacts on security prices by purchasing securities of companies that are fallen angels or turnaround candidates. The surprise of a business downturn is lessened because this condition pre-exists and is already reflected in the security price paid. In other words, most of the bad news is out; more bad news cannot do much additional harm to the security price.

Interest rate risk is a very real concern for total return investors. The prices of all stocks respond to broad movements in the interest rate level because of its impact on economic activity and the business outlook. As interest rates move up, fixed-income securities become a more attractive investment alternative to stocks. Funds move out of the stock market and into the bond market.

Generally speaking, when interest rates rise, stock prices drop. Investors perceive that higher interest rates will choke the economy and hurt corporate earnings. Investors move money from the stock market to the bond market in search of higher yields; this has a depressing effect on stock prices.

The prices of many high-yielding stocks, such as telephone companies, banks, real estate investment trusts and electric utilites, are more sensitive to changes in interest rates than are other stocks. Witness what happened during April 1987, when rates shot up in an attempt by the Federal Reserve to defend the weak U.S. dollar in international markets. The Dow-Jones utility share averages declined by 15% in a very short period of time, while the stock market as a whole dipped only slightly.

Because the total return derived from high-yielding stocks is made up of about two-thirds current income and one-third capital appreciation, a majority of the expected total return from these securities will be related to happenings in the fixed-income market. With modest capital appreciation and dividend growth features, these stocks are often looked upon as alternatives to fixed-income investments. Yet they're susceptible to similar interest rate risks as bonds, although not to the same degree.

All bonds are subject to interest rate risk—the risk that interest rates will rise and the bond prices will drop. Small movements in interest rates can wipe out capital appreciation in a hurry. But the type of bonds total return investors purchase—discount bonds—usually sell more on the business prospects of the issuer, rather than in response to changes in interest rate levels. Minor fluctuations in interest rates have little effect on their prices. And convertible bond prices are mainly governed by the action of the underlying stock price, and will not be as affected by interest rate movements as will the price of a straight bond.

Notwithstanding what was said above, there's no question of the correlation between interest rate movements and prices of the type of securities that total return investors purchase. Don't be led into a false sense of security that total return investors are, for some reason, free of any interest rate risk, or for that matter, other investment risks. The objective is to control risk through proper security selection and portfolio composition.

The next chapter explains certain principles you must follow to become the complete total return investor.

Chapter 3

Principles of Total Return Investing

As a prospective total return investor, you must adhere to several important principles in order to profit from this strategy. These include looking for relative investment value, purchasing securities with above-average yields, diversifying your portfolio properly, and exercising patience. Together, these key principles form an investment philosophy that will put you on the path to prosperity.

First and foremost, to be a successful total return investor, you must look for relative values among all major investment areas, picking those that offer the most promising returns in the long run. Second, you should emphasize current yield as much as capital appreciation, with at least one-third to one-half of your total return coming from current income, although this will vary according to each investor's own circumstances. Third, you should diversify your holdings adequately to protect against unforeseen problems with any investment. Fourth, you need to exercise a patient buy-and-hold philosophy, as opposed to constant trading in hopes of quick profits.

Look for Relative Value

Any astute investor knows not to follow the fad of the moment, but rather to try and ascertain the next trend before it becomes popular. You can't follow the herd and end up in the winner's circle. The total return investor looks for relative value among all potential investment areas, including stocks, bonds, real estate, money market equivalents, and even precious metals (through dividend-paying stocks).

Investing follows the laws of supply and demand. Most persons want to jump on the bandwagon and purchase what everyone else is buying. They unwittingly fall into the "greater fool" syndrome, which means that you don't worry about the price you're paying, because there's always someone who'll pay more later on. Many fell into this trap as the Dow crossed 2700 in August 1987, but then plunged 1000 points in less than two months. Greed quickly turned to fear.

Stockbrokers and financial planners always find it easier to sell securities that everyone wants to buy as opposed to the ones that are out-of-favor. Investment money has a tendency to flow to those areas with the perceived highest return. The key word is "perceived." The perception is based on history, and in the financial markets history rarely repeats itself. What was profitable yesterday or is a money-maker today, may not be so tomorrow. Unfortunately for many investors, expected returns often differ from the returns finally realized.

The very act of buying into areas where future returns appear to be the greatest increases the demand for and bids up the cost of the investment, thus reducing total returns. Witness the classic case of the oil industry in the early 1980s. When oil was at $30 a barrel and a sure bet to rise to $100, investment funds poured in. Drilling activity shot up and so did costs as many dollars chased the few available oil rigs and crews. The result was predictible—overproduction. Prices fell and investors lost a bundle of money in the oil patch.

The same phenomenon happened to the real estate industry in many sections of the country during the early 1980s. With easy credit supplied by the savings and loan industry, investors seeking generous tax breaks, and a history of rising real estate prices, it was an easy game to play. As overbuilding ensued and vacancy rates soared, rents softened and owners of leveraged properties developed cash flow problems. This downward cycle produced negative returns for many investors—not only were cash flows in the red, but property values actually shrunk.

Depressed sectors represent excellent investment opportunities for the total return investor. Low investment costs now often mean high returns later. Easy money can be made by wise investors who put funds into areas that are unpopular, where the cost of investment entry has declined, and above all, where projected returns are high if the sector turns around.

The current situation in the oil and gas industry is a case in point. Production is down, reserves are cheap, and the cost of drilling has nosedived, making new oil and gas investments very attractive to those investors willing to wait for the eventual recovery of prices. And it will come sooner or later.

An example of a successful turnaround was the cable TV industry of a few years ago, when pessimism pervaded the investment community. Cost overruns in the big cities, high turnoff rates, and problems with overbidding for new franchises plagued the industry. Cable TV systems sold for less than $1,000 per subscriber in 1983. By 1987, thanks to cable deregulation and other factors, system prices had been bid up to over $2,000 a subscriber. Those who had invested during the pessimistic years could now sell out at substantial profits.

As cable TV systems prices soared, money began to pour into cable TV investments with the talk of deregulation, system growth, and high profits. In the first quarter of 1987, sales of cable TV public limited partnerships showed the greatest increase of any partnership category, running at an annual rate of eight times that of 1984 ($800 million versus $100 million). The public was clearly in a buying mood thanks to talk of easy profits. How long the euphoria will last is anyone's guess now that system prices have been bid up out of sight.

How does the total return investor search for relative value? You need to compare the expected returns available from various types of securities representing different segments of the economy. What is the difference in current yields among stocks, convertible bonds, discount straight bonds, Treasury bills, real estate, and oil and gas? What premiums are being paid for future growth of income? What are the prospects for capital appreciation given recent performance history? What are the risks that current income will be cut or capital appreciation won't be realized? The securities with the best expected total return (or conversely, the most undervalued ones) are the ones to invest in.

You might want to construct a chart similar to that shown in Table 1 (page 28). Based on the results in this hypothetical list of expected total returns, adjusted for risk, you'd make an effort to move capital into discount bonds, real estate, and oil and gas. They offer the best investment returns. Your portfolio should be weighted toward these areas.

You or your advisors need to construct your own chart and consult it from time to time. You'll have to rethink what your expected total returns are for each investment area and make portfolio adjustments when necessary. Relative returns change over time. Therefore, you must be in a position to respond accordingly to maintain the investment edge.

Table 1: Expected Total Returns for Various Investment Areas

	Current Returns	Capital Apprec.	Total Returns
Stocks	5%	2%	7%
Convertible bonds	6	2	8
Discount bonds	10	5	15
Long-term bonds	8	0	8
Treasury bills	6	0	6
Real estate	8	3	11
Oil and Gas	10	3	13
Gold	0	8	8

Invest for Above-Average Yield

A total return portfolio of stocks, bonds and other securities should produce a yield at least 50% higher than the S&P 500 average stock yield. Higher-yielding securities contribute several benefits to your total return portfolio. First, they provide downside protection against a general drop in security prices because their yield acts to support the price. In a market slide of 25%, stocks with above-average dividend yields and good prospects for dividend increases should drop only 10% to 15%.

The second benefit is that high-yielding securities usually have lower betas than the market and their price movements are less volatile than those of pure growth securities. With lower price-earnings ratios, they're less expensive in terms of what investors pay for each dollar of earnings. As a result, negative surprises have less impact on their stock prices.

Finally, high-yielding securities increase the current return component of the total return equation, making total return projections more reliable. Cash dividends and interest payments are more certain than security price appreciation. A dollar of income today is worth more than a dollar of capital gain tomorrow.

Plenty of common stocks of solid, conservative companies provide relatively high yields. These include natural gas distributors, electric utilities, telephone companies, international oil companies, money center banks, as well as real estate investment trusts and master limited partnerships. Many of these high-yielding stocks also have good capital gain possibilities.

The *Value Line Investment Survey's* publishes a list of the highest yielding non-utility stocks based on estimated year-ahead dividends. A number of these stocks are of companies in the above-named industry groups. Stocks of fallen angel companies appear on the list as well. A wide range is available to select from.

It isn't difficult to find convertible securities or discount straight bonds with current yields 50% or greater than the S&P 500 averages. Just about all of them offer good yields. However, when yields on these debt securities are higher than normal, the total return investor must look closely at the issuing company's financials to determine the stability of interest payments. Lofty yields are often associated with high risk and scare many investors.

On the other hand, moderately high yields don't necessarily translate into high risk. Take, for instance, public utility companies that pay out a large percent of earnings to stockholders as dividends. Because they're not perceived as pure growth companies, their stocks are reasonably priced. Although they sport dividend yields which are often 50% to 100% higher than the market average, they have high-quality ratings and a history of low price volatility.

Table 2 (page 30) compares historical yields of the Standard & Poor's 400 industrial stocks with yields of the S&P 40 utility stocks.

In every year, yields for the utilities were at least 50% higher; in some years they were more than double the 400 industrial average. This is an impressive yield advantage for utility stocks and the investors who purchase them.

High-yielding utility stocks can also provide excellent total returns, especially when their dividends increase each year. A prime example is the stock of Connecticut Energy Corporation, formerly known as the Southern Connecticut Gas Company, which carries a 7% dividend yield. Shareholders of this NYSE-listed gas distribution company have earned a 10-year compound annual total return of 18.0% between 1977 and 1986. This compares to the S&P 500's return of only 13.6% for the same period.

Although Connecticut Energy has had a spotty earnings record, its service area is growing and the company is branching out into new business ventures. The source of the solid total return performance comes from its strong dividend record. Not only has Connecticut Energy increased

Table 2

Year	Yields * S&P 400	Util. 40	Difference in Yields
1977	4.9%	7.4%	51%
1978	5.0	8.9	78
1979	4.9	9.3	90
1980	4.2	9.5	126
1981	5.1	10.0	96
1982	4.6	9.6	109
1983	4.0	9.1	128
1984	4.0	8.5	113
1985	3.3	7.2	118
1986	3.4	6.3	85

*Percents shown are average yields during the last month of each year.

dividend payments every year since 1975, it has also paid cash dividends since 1850—the longest consecutive dividend record of any non-financial company listed on the New York Stock Exchange.

A few stocks have abnormally high yields because of market fears that the dividend will be cut or eliminated. Bonds have high yields because of concern that interest payments won't be made on them. Market prices already reflect these fears and concerns. Stated yields are based on prior dividend and interest payments. Higher than market yields reflect the uncertainty of future payouts. If and when adverse action finally occurs on the payout, further price declines can be expected.

After all the bad news is out, a few daring total return investors will buy the distressed company's securities in the hopes that payments will eventually be restored in full. If correct in their analysis, they'll profit handsomely from their boldness because the stock or bond price will surely rebound. These savvy investors capture both the added income and capital appreciation.

Several years ago, Kansas Gas and Electric Company ran into problems with its state regulatory agencies over including the costs of Wolf Creek Station, a huge nuclear plant, in its rate base. Although the plant was operationally safe and sound, construction costs turned out to be enormous and state authorities didn't want to raise electric rates by prohibitive amounts.

When all the negatives were obvious to everyone, the company announced it was cutting the dividend in half from $2.36 to $1.18 per share. The stock nosedived from $15 down to $9.63 a share in October, 1985. Even with the much lower dividend, the yield was a generous 12.3%. It appeared to be a perfect time for daring total return investors to purchase KG&E shares.

And they made the right move. In a little over a year the company took steps to cut overhead, shore up its finances, and successfully bring the Wolf Creek nuclear plant on stream. In November, 1986, KG&E directors raised the quarterly dividend by 15% and announced that they were committed to restoring it completely to former levels. By year-end, the utility's bond ratings were upgraded and the stock price had bounced all the way back up to $23. Needless to say, this is the type of scenario that total return investors thrive on—double-digit current yields and triple-digit capital appreciation.

Diversify Portfolio

The main problem with purchasing individual stocks and bonds for a total return portfolio is that you can't properly diversify when total funds in your account are small. If your portfolio consists of equal amounts of just three securities and the price of one drops in half, your total portfolio value will suffer a 16.7% loss. Even with as many as five securities, the loss is 10%.

Table 3 shows what happens as you add securities to your holdings.

As might be expected, the more you own, the less total risk in the portfolio. This assumes that equal amounts of each security are purchased and no two are securities of companies in the same industry. After you own six, the risk reduction caused by adding one more security diminishes from 5% to 2%; after the tenth holding, an extra five securities reduces portfolio risk by a total of only 5%.

Simply put, the greatest decrease in portfolio risk occurs when the first few securities are added. As more are purchased, portfolio risk continues to fall, albeit at decreasing rates. This is better illustrated by Figure 1 (page 33), where the total risk curve flattens out after 15 securities are in the portfolio.

Table 3

Number of Issues in Portfolio	Percent of Total Risk	Percent by Which Risk Reduced	Cumulative Risk Reduction
1	100%	0%	0%
2	80	20	20
3	75	5	25
4	70	5	30
5	65	5	35
6	60	5	40
7	58	2	42
8	56	2	44
9	54	2	46
10	52	2	48
15	47	5	53
20	45%	2%	55%

Table 3 and Figure 1 indicate you'll need securities of at least 10 companies in different industries to have an adequate amount of diversification—15 would be ideal. At first blush, this suggests having at least a $20,000 to $25,000 portfolio before you consider purchasing individual stocks and bonds. However, with a total return portfolio, your minimum number of securities might be even lower because they aren't as volatile as other securities.

A total return investor could possibly get by with $10,000 invested in only four or five securities. In this situation, you'd want to take a conservative tack by orienting the security selections to solid companies with good financial histories and above-average earnings prospects. However, because they'll be fairly priced in an efficient market (i.e., few growth stock bargains usually exist unless the market itself is oversold), your expected total return will be lower.

Total return investors purchasing high-yield securities of fallen angels or financially unstable companies in anticipation of higher returns need a greater measure of diversification for these riskier investments. At least

Figure 1

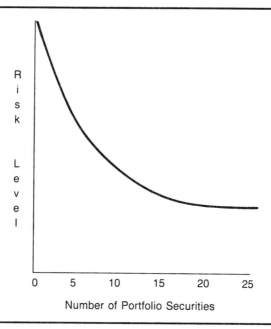

Number of Portfolio Securities

$20,000 to $25,000 split among 8 to 10 investments in different industries would normally suffice. An ideal portfolio size would be $50,000 spread among 20 securities. That way, if the fortunes of one company go from bad to worse, the total return investor is in a good position to weather a loss.

Most persons with less than $10,000 to invest will be best off purchasing mutual funds employing the total return philosophy. Mutual funds offer instant diversification—a portfolio of 25 to several hundred securities—which mitigates business and industry risk. Appropriate total return funds include equity-income funds, some growth and income funds, and convertible bond funds. Any fund that has as its core strategy investing in dividend-paying common stocks and convertible securities will fit the total return bill.

Exercise Patience

As an investor, you must presume that over the long term the American economy will expand and create investment opportunities along the way.

In the short run, however, the financial markets will continue to show varying degrees of volatility, with interest rates moving up and down, the inflation rate changing, and stock and bond prices rising and falling. These fluctuations cannot be predicted or timed with any meaningful accuracy.

Total return investors must exercise patience in order for this strategy to work. It takes time before total returns are realized, either through a steady growth of earnings and dividends of a strong company, or the price recovery of the stock or bond of a financially weak company. As part of this discipline, the total return investor must be willing to ride out small movements in securities prices. Attention must be focused on the end result—realized capital appreciation—not on short-term price swings.

Total return investors are rewarded for their patience. They get an immediate, steady stream of cash dividends and interest payments while they wait to garner long-term gains. As the income stream increases and becomes more certain from stronger cash flows, higher security prices are likely to follow. The income engine drives the vehicle known as capital appreciation. Again, this chain of events takes time—don't expect to double your money in less than a year using the total return approach.

If you're buying a growth stock or a convertible bond of a growth company—one whose dividend increases every year and whose share price will hopefully also go up in response to higher earnings and dividends—then plan on holding that security at least five years. Under normal circumstances, this will take you through a business cycle and a bull and bear stock market.

If you plan on buying the security of a financially distressed or out-of-favor company, count on a two to two-and-a-half year wait, at a minimum, for a turnaround to occur. It often takes this much time for new management to straighten the business out or for cyclical businesses to right themselves. With some industries such as the banking, real estate, and restaurant chain businesses, the wait for an upturn may be even longer.

In other situations you'll be rewarded quickly for your astuteness in total return investing—the security will reach your appreciation objectives much sooner than you expected. Proceed to accelerate your timetable. In this case, you sell when your price objective for the security is met regardless of how long you've held it. Then move on to pick your next portfolio winner.

The following chapters discuss specific total return securities, the benefits they provide, and the role they play in the total return scheme of things. The next chapter explains how to use common stocks as total return securities in your portfolio.

Chapter 4

Chapter 6

Investing in Total Return Stocks

Investors may choose between two general approaches to purchasing common stocks for total return. The first approach is to pursue a growth stock strategy based on an increasing stream of dividends; the second involves buying undervalued, out-of-favor, or fallen angel stocks. Before beginning a discussion of the different strategies, it will be helpful to review how common stocks are valued in the marketplace.

Common Stock Valuation Theory

A well-known theory is that the price of a stock equals the present value of its future stream of dividends or earnings. In other words, future dividends are discounted to their present value and the sum of these represents the share price an investor should be willing to pay for them.

With interest rates remaining at 10%, the present value of a dollar to be received in five years is $.62. Reversing the process, if you took today's $.62 and invested it at 10%, it will be worth exactly one dollar in five years. The rationale is that a dollar today is worth more than a dollar tommorrow—it is certain, you can earn interest on it, and it will grow in value, whereas a dollar tommorrow will be worth just that—a dollar.

Translating this present value theory into stock pricing theory is done by taking a stream of future dividends and discounting each year's dividend to the present using an appropriate market interest rate. Often this is the rate for riskless, short-term Treasury bills or a one-year U.S. government note.

How do you predict what the future stream of dividends will be? The simplest and often best yardstick is past history. Take a company's recent earnings and dividend data and extrapolate it into the future using an appropriate growth rate. Examine the company's prior record to look for yearly variations in earnings and dividend payout ratios and factor this into your projections, along with any other knowledge you might have about the company's prospects.

The stock ought to sell for the sum of the present value of all future dividends. If it's higher, then the stock is overpriced and should be avoided. If the stock sells below the sum of the discounted future dividends, then it should be considered for purchase. This arithmetic is illustrated by the following equations, where it's assumed that the dividends increase at 6% a year.

Future Year Dividends

Year	1	2	3	4	5	6 ....
V =	$1.00 +	$1.06 +	$1.12 +	$1.19 +	$1.26 +	$1.34 + ...

V is the current value of the stock and the numbers to the right of the equal sign represent the future stream of annual dividends that the common stock will generate for the investor. This future stream must be discounted to its present value by using an appropriate interest rate such as 10%. This is shown in the equation below. Solving for PV (the present value), the stock is worth $35.33. This is the theoretical value based on the discounted stream of future dividends.

Future Year Discounted Dividends

Year	1	2	3	4	5	6
PV =	$0.91 +	$0.88 +	$0.84 +	$0.81 +	$0.78 +	$0.75 +

$30.36 (sum of all dividends in years thereafter)
PV = $35.33

If the stock sells at $30 a share, then an opportunity for capital appreciation is present. If the stock is priced at $40 a share, this indicates an overvalued situation you'd want to avoid. Naturally, it's difficult to predict a future stream of dividends. The further out you go, the less certain the dividend stream is and the more imprecise the predictions become. Appendix A of this book lists some present value tables to use when you want to run your own calculations for certain stocks.

Growth Stock Total Return Strategy

The growth stock strategy is exactly what the name implies. Investors seek stocks that have good earnings histories and dividend growth records, buy them, and hold them for the long term. As the earnings and dividends continue to increase, the price of the stock, hopefully, will move upwards. Higher dividends reflect the confidence management has in the company's future. The total return investor benefits from both greater current dividend income and possible capital appreciation.

Pure growth stock investors find happiness in a stock that doubles within a year. Students of the more conservative total return philosophy are satisfied with dividends doubling in ten years (a 7% compound annual growth rate). They're ecstatic if they find a company that triples its dividend in ten years (a 12% growth rate).

A problem with the growth stock strategy is that companies whose sales and earnings are growing faster then average usually payout only a small percentage of earnings in dividends. Current yields are low. For the total return investor, this means a greater reliance on more speculative capital gain income. Except in unusual circumstances, total return investors shouldn't be interested in the stocks of companies that pay no dividends; they're best owned by investors who follow a the pure growth philosophy.

The total return investor occasionally finds a smaller company with good growth prospects that pays a dividend. Its shares might be hidden in the bowels of the over-the-counter market. Often the company is in a less glamorous industry and isn't followed by Wall Street research departments. It's been neglected by institutional investors because of its small capitalization and a thin trading market for the stock. They can't buy or sell in size without disrupting the market. As these small companies grow and gain the market recognition they deserve, they may wind up as good total return investments. However, most of the return will have to come from the less certain capital appreciation component.

Effect of Price-Earnings Changes

Changes in a stock's price-earnings ratio (P/E ratio) are also a determinant of total return. The P/E ratio, sometimes referred to as the stock's "multiple," is the price paid for $1 in earnings. A P/E ratio of 12 indicates the stock is selling for 12 times its earnings per share. As a rule of thumb, stocks with higher price-earnings ratios are perceived by the market as having greater growth prospects. Investors are willing to pay more now for their future stream of income.

For the total return concept to work with growth stocks, the price-earnings (P/E) ratio of the stock must either stay the same or move upwards. If it contracts, it will invariably cut into total returns. Table 1 shows what happens to the price of a stock when the multiple stays the same, increases, and decreases, assuming corporate earnings move up in each of three years.

Table 1: Effect of Price-Earnings Changes on Share Price

	Year		
	1	2	3
Earnings per share	$1.00	$1.10	$1.25
Same price-earnings multiple	10	10	10
Share price	$10.00	$11.00	$12.50
Increasing P/E multiple	10	11	12
Share price	$10.00	$12.10	$15.00
Decreasing P/E multiple	10	9	8
Share price	$10.00	$9.90	$10.00

With a decreasing multiple, the share price drops in the second year to $9.90 and recovers to $10 in year three, even though earnings are increasing in each of those years. No capital appreciation takes place. At $10, its price is still quite a bit less than the $12.50 and $15 results achieved under the other two scenarios.

Simply put, total return stock investors do not need P/E multiple expansion to succeed; they do very well as long as per share earnings and dividends are increasing and the stock's multiple stays the same. However, if for one reason or another the price-earnings ratio increases along with earnings, then the stock price will move up at an even faster pace. This is the best of both worlds.

The Marriot Corporation is a prime example of a growth company whose earnings, dividends and price-earnings ratio have all grown in recent years. Aggressive total return investors willing to bet on this extremely successful food and lodging company have been well-rewarded. Look at the impressive numbers presented in Table 2.

Table 2: Marriot Corporation Financial History
(Year-end December 31)

	1981	1982	1983	1984	1985	1986
Earnings	$ .57	$ .61	$ .78	$ 1.00	$ 1.24	$ 1.40
Dividend	$ .05	$ .06	$ .08	$ .09	$ .11	$ .14
Yield *	0.8%	0.8%	0.7%	0.6%	0.7%	0.7%
Year-end price	$ 7.18	$11.70	$14.25	$14.70	$21.58	$29.75
P-E ratio	12.6	19.2	18.3	14.7	17.4	21.3
Price increase **	13.1%	63.0%	21.8%	3.2%	46.8%	37.9%
Total Return	13.9%	63.8%	22.5%	3.8%	47.5%	38.6%

*Calculated by dividing the dividend by the prior year's closing price.
**Calculated by dividing the increase in price during the year by the prior year's closing price.

The Marriot Corporation is a well-managed company with a strong franchise and an awesome earnings record. Investors who held the stock for the 1982-1986 period averaged 31.7% annual total returns. Most of this came from capital appreciation driven by earnings growth and a price-earning multiple expansion from 12.6 to 21.3.

Dividends increased at a large percentage rate, more than doubling in the last five years. Although Marriot's current yield of 0.7% and dividend payout ratio of 10% of earnings are quite low, this is typical of a fast-growing company. The bulk of earnings is plowed back into fixed assets and working capital to finance future growth.

How long Marriot can sustain this record is anyone's guess. Judging from the price-earnings ratio, investors are betting on increased earnings and dividends from the corporation for some time to come. The key problem for total return growth investors is timing the sale of their stock before a slowdown in growth becomes apparent, causing a contraction in the price-earnings multiple.

The P/E ratio of any stock could drop for a variety of reasons. There might be an investor perception of a lower rate of earnings growth, the quality of earnings may deteriorate, or the industry may become out-of-favor with Wall Steet. Take the example of NCNB Corporation, formerly known as the North Carolina National Bank.

As the largest bank in the southeast and the 16th largest in the country, NCNB's recent record is one of solid earnings growth. Yet like many banks, its price-earnings ratio is much lower than the average of all stocks in the S&P 500 index. Table 3 presents NCNB's record since 1981, expressed in per share figures and adjusted for stock splits.

Table 3:   NCNB Financial History (Year-end December 31)

	1981	1982	1983	1984	1985	1986
Earnings	$ 1.23	$ 1.54	$ 1.77	$ 1.96	$ 2.30	$ 2.53
Dividend	$ .41	$ .46	$ .52	$ .59	$ .69	$ .78
Yield *	5.9%	5.5%	4.3%	3.8%	3.4%	3.9%
Year-end price	$ 7.50	$ 9.38	$13.75	$18.00	$22.63	$21.50
P-E ratio	6.0	6.1	7.8	9.2	9.8	8.5
Price increase**	15.4%	25.1%	46.6%	30.9%	25.7%	-5.0%
Total Return	21.3%	30.5%	50.9%	34.7%	29.1%	-1.1%

*Calculated by dividing the dividend by the prior year's closing price.
**Calculated by dividing the increase in price during the year by the prior year's closing price.

NCNB Corporation's stock achieved remarkably good total returns for investors between 1982 and 1985, averaging 32% annually during these years. However, in spite of increased earnings in 1986, the stock price slid backwards by the end of the year, reducing the total return to a minus 1.1%. (Notice, however, that this return would have been even worse had not the dividend yield contributed positively to it.)

The problem was that bank stocks lost investor appeal in 1986, which was reflected in lower price-earnings ratios for the industry. NCNB was no exception. Its P/E ratio dropped from 9.8 to 8.5 during that year, after having climbed each of the previous four years.

Overpaying for Growth

Unfortunately, most large capitalization growth companies are well-known to investors and Wall Street analysts who report on them. Their excellent financial histories are available to everyone. Investors are willing to pay more for a faster growing company than for a slow growing one, as evidenced by the high price-earnings ratios that former companies carry. In an efficient market, publicly available information is already reflected in the share price. This assumes that investors act rationally.

An extreme example of how overpaying for growth got out of hand occurred back in the early 1970s when what was known as the "nifty-fifty" investment strategy was in vogue with professional money managers. It was believed that a group of about 50 high-growth, low dividend-paying stocks were "one decision" stocks. That is, you bought them, held them, and watched as the earnings, dividends, and stock prices went up forever. You never had to worry about selling them.

The net result of heavy institutional buying and virtually no selling pressure was that the prices of many of these nifty-fifty stocks were eventually bid up to 40 to 50 times earnings, three to four times the market averages. They included familiar corporate names such as IBM, Xerox, Avon Products, Johnson and Johnson, and Minnesota Mining.

The nifty-fifty investing concept was shattered with the bear market of 1974-5. The stock prices of many of these companies dropped by half, creating significant investment losses for their owners. And they were a long time in recovering. This scenario was typical of two common mistakes made by many growth stock investors: they pay too much for current earnings and over-estimate the growth of future earnings.

The nifty-fifty era of stock market history demonstrates that very few good things go on forever, especially in the competitive world of business and finance. As all economists know, high rates of return attract competitors. IBM and Xerox, once giants of their booming industries, have found this out. Furthermore, high rates of growth eventually slow as markets mature. Being caught holding stocks of companies when the music stops is a major risk of total return investing in growth stocks.

The total return growth investor must always be prepared to accept the risk of lower multiples of earnings when the corporate growth rate slows down. As shown previously, contracting multiples usually mean lower stock prices and reduced or non-existent total returns, even though the dividends may still be rising because the company pays out a higher percentage of earnings as it matures. This notion of a slowdown in earnings and shrinking of multiples during the corporate maturation process can be illustrated in Figure 1.

Figure 1: Earnings, Price and P-E Ratio of Maturing Company

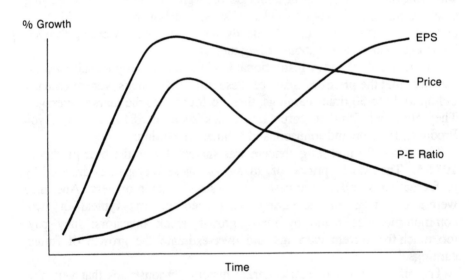

Total return investors must avoid buying in at the top by overpaying for the stock of a company that has seen its best growth period. If the price drops, then the expected total return could easily become a negative figure, particularly when the common stock yield is very low. Keep in mind that with growth stock investing, a high percent of the total return is expected to come from the capital appreciation component in the total return equation.

The one bright spot is that higher current yields should provide some support for the share price. As the growth line slows, the company may begin to pay out a larger share of earnings as dividends—it doesn't need as much earnings to finance growth. Or it may begin a share repurchase program. The company may feel that at this stage in its life cycle its shareholders can do a better job investing corporate earnings than it can. As dividend payments increase, this adds to total returns and helps support the price of the stock. With non-dividend paying, pure growth stocks, the price adjustment to an earnings slowdown will likely be much more severe.

Share Repurchases

Many companies are in the market repurchasing shares they believe to be undervalued. Their stocks merit the attention of total return investors. Repurchases are an alternative to paying extra dividends to shareholders. In fact, they're becoming so popular that conservative corporations including General Motors, Hewlett-Packard, Merck, ITT, Anheuser-Busch, Firestone, GAF, and Tektronix are going this route to rid themselves of excess liquidity. And they're boosting share prices, at least in the period shortly after the repurchase decision.

Before a buy-back can commence, management needs permission from its Board of Directors and must publicly announce the action to comply with SEC rules. Often the purchases are made over a period of time so as not to affect the price of the stock. In other cases, the company buys its shares though a tender offer. It offers to pay a set price at a premium to the market as an inducement to shareholders to tender stock. It engages a brokerage firm to buy a specific number of tendered shares on its behalf.

Companies who repurchase their stock have excess liquidity and might chose to raise the dividend. But they don't want to increase it to a rate that may not be sustainable in future years. Yet a special cash dividend accomplishes very little because it's a one-time event with little positive impact on share price.

On the other hand, the stock repurchase route brings several benefits. First, it provides price support for the common stock by soaking up excess supply. Second, it gives a boost to earnings per share by reducing the number of shares outstanding. Third, it reduces total dividend payments required in the future, because they'll be paid on fewer common shares.

Companies instituting stock repurchases are often good investments for total return devotees. They have good cash flows and pay relatively high dividends. With fewer shares receiving dividends, it's easier for the company to raise the payout in subsequent years. All this should add up to price appreciation for total return investors. An important consideration is to begin your purchases after the company completes its repurchasing so you're not competing with it on the specialist's order book.

A corporation shouldn't pay more for its stock than it's worth—the true value of its business. It should buy when the market price is depressed. In the aftermath of the October 1987 stock market crash, dozens of companies announced repurchase programs to take advantage of what they perceived were extraordinarily cheap prices.

It should be pointed out that companies with very high price-earnings ratios who buy back their stock may actually dilute earnings. And buybacks increase risks to total return investors, particularly if they're financed with debt. The company may find it needs the cash reserves at a future date to tide it over a cyclical downturn in business. Therefore, carefully choose your investments in companies that have completed a share repurchase program.

Value-Oriented Strategy

Another basic approach to investing in total return stocks is to use a value-oriented strategy, where you buy into so-called fallen angel companies or stocks that have been ignored by other investors. Or perhaps you purchase shares of a company that's in an unpopular industry, or where an outside factor has had an unfavorable impact on its near-term prospects.

Some call this value-oriented approach a contrarian investing philosophy. Others call it "bottom fishing"—searching for stocks that have hit rock bottom. Whatever its name, total return investors pursuing this strategy must be willing to go against the tide of popular opinion, purchase the stock, and then have the patience to wait for the financial turnaround to transpire and the negative feelings to pass. When this occurs, contrarians will be amply rewarded with higher portfolio values.

On the surface it appears logical to want to purchase shares of companies that have a good earnings record and prospects for the same, and not buy into companies with poor records whose problems are obvious to all. In other words, why not follow the investing crowd and buy popular stocks and ignore the unpopular ones? Logically, it would appear more profitable to jump on the bandwagon, ride with the upward momentum, and get out at the top.

The problem with this approach is that investors tend to bid up the prices of popular stocks and sell unpopular ones. The net result is that popular stocks are overpriced and out-of-favor ones are often underpriced. This is the same as buying high and selling low, an outcome that rarely makes money for any investor. Unfortunately, this is the basic market psychology that both individual and institutional investors employ. Fortunately, it creates unusual profit opportunities for advocates of the total return philosophy.

From a total return standpoint, investing in undervalued stocks has several merits. Most importantly, it's a buy-low, sell-high philosophy designed to produce capital gains. Usually, investors have overreacted to negative news and the stocks are over-sold in an inefficient market. Conventional money ignores these opportunities; smart money capitalizes on them.

Out-of-favor stocks usually have good dividend yields. This puts a floor under the price as long as the company has the financial resources to continue the payout. Furthermore, the risk of further stock price drops is less because the market has usually discounted all the bad news. If the company turns itself around, there's a good chance that the dividend will go up, particularly when it hasn't been increased for several years.

Here's a story of a stock that typifies the problems of the growth stock theory of total return investing and points up opportunities for value-oriented, contrarian investors. The name of the company is Lomas and Nettleton Financial Corporation and its stock trades on the Big Board. It's in the mortgage banking industry, providing financial services to the real estate industry, mortgages to home buyers, mortgage loan originations, administration services to institutional investors, and a host of other financial services.

L&N Financial had a long, uninterrupted string of earnings and dividend increases. Having produced an average annual total return of 47.2%, it appeared to be the perfect total return holding for those investors with a penchant for growth stocks. Furthermore, it paid out a large percentage of profits to stockholders and always carried a relatively low price-earnings ratio, which is unusual for a growth company (see Table 4).

Table 4: Lomas and Nettleton Financial History
(Year-end June 30th)

	1982	1983	1984	1985	1986
Earnings	$ 1.01	$1.27	$ 1.57	$ 1.87	$ 2.19
Dividend	$ .49	$ .57	$ .69	$ .81	$ .97
Yield *	6.3%	3.2%	4.4%	3.5%	3.2%
Year-end price 6/30	$ 7.75	$17.85	$15.60	$23.00	$33.34
P-E ratio	7.7	14.1	10.0	12.3	15.2
Price increase **	5.4%	130.3%	-12.6%	47.4%	45.0%
Total Return	11.7%	133.5%	-8.2%	50.9%	48.2%

*Calculated by dividing the dividend by the prior year's closing price.
**Calculated by dividing the increase in price during the year by the prior year's closing price.

Everything was going along smoothly until the third quarter of fiscal year 1987, when Lomas management decided to take a $25 million write-off for bad debts. Actually, there was a hint of coming losses in the fiscal year 1986 annual report with references to "storm clouds on the horizon" and the fact that management expected losses from foreclosures to increase from $800,000 in 1986 to $3.5 million in 1987.

The $25 million write-off reduced earnings for the quarter and the year. Management put its best foot foward and showed its confidence in the future by voting a 25% increase in the annual dividend. Notwithstanding, the stock reacted by skidding from a high of $39.25 in March, 1987 down to the $25 per share range in several months. Earnings estimates of $2.50 a share were scaled back to $2.20.

The question remaining is can L&N Financial recover from the bad debt losses and pick up where it left off? At $25 the stock yielded 5.6%, double the S&P 500 average yield, and sold at a price-earnings ratio of only 50% of the market multiple. If the turnaround occurs, investors with an eye on fallen angels may profit from ownership of Lomas and Nettleton shares as did growth stock total return investors of yesteryear.

Low Price-Earnings Multiple Stocks

The search for bargain issues involves two different approaches to security analysis. The first is the price-earnings or capitalization approach, where the stock looks undervalued based on the multiplier applied to future earnings. In other words, if you find a stock which you believe has earning power 50% greater than is reflected in the price, you may have a bargain. Likewise, any stock selling for 25% less than the market's price-earnings ratio may offer good value, assuming earnings continue to grow.

By investing in low-multiple, total return stocks, you get a chance for a double gain when you're right. The stock price moves up both from an increase in earnings and an upward revision of the multiple. For instance, if earnings increase from $1.00 a share to $1.25 and the multiple moves from 10 to 12, the share price will rise from $10 to $15 for a 50% gain. Had only the earnings increased, the stock would have gone from $10 to $12.50 for a much smaller 25% gain.

An example of this phenomenon occurred with the share price of Eastman Kodak, a former "nifty-fifty" company from the early 1970s. Its stock sold as high as $101 in 1972, but plunged to below $30 by 1978. For years Kodak was viewed as an aging giant in a mature industry. Diversification efforts were a mixed bag. EK shares sold at a discount to the market's average price-earnings ratio.

Then all of a sudden Kodak's stock began to move in mid-1986 as quarterly earnings comparisons improved. It rose from the high $40s to over $100 in one year. The stock's price-earnings ratio went from a discount to the market to a slight premium. What was the reason behind Wall Street's sudden bullishness on Kodak's stock? It was caused by a boost in sales of 35mm film which in turn was triggered by the introduction of a new automatic-focus 35mm camera and the advent of the one-hour photo finishing industry.

The tipoff on the turnaround in earnings actually came in 1985 when Kodak announced a huge write-off after it gave up the ghost on its instant film business. This eventually totaled $500 million. At the same time, the company also said it planned to cut its workforce 10% and slash expenses another 5%.

With all the negatives out on the table and a relatively low price-earnings ratio, savy total return investors who focused on the 5% dividend yield and the company's bright prospects bought in and waited. Their total returns reached the 100% annual rate, thanks to both per share earnings increases and an upward multiple revision of Kodak's stock.

Asset Value Approach

Another value-oriented approach to total return stock investing is to look at a company's asset values; if the stock is selling at less than book value per share, then it may be a bargain. Book value (also called net worth or shareholders' equity) is simply the difference between a corporation's assets and liabilities divided by the number of common shares outstanding. If a stock sells for less than net working capital per share (current assets less current liabilities divided by number of shares) then it's probably even a better bargain.

The Value Line Investment Survey prepares lists of those stocks it follows whose shares sell at the widest price discount to book value. They range from 19% to 92% and there's plenty of them available for total return investors. You need to determine the "whys and wherefores" for these discrepancies between price and book value and then be ready to act on those stocks that appear to be cheap.

Persons who purchased Gulf & Western stock at less than book value back in early 1983 had plenty to crow about while they watched the share price double by early 1986 and quadruple by 1987. And as though that weren't enough, the dividend went up by 33% during this time—quite a total return story for those who specialize in asset value investing.

At the end of 1982, G&W's book value was $28 per share. Yet the stock was selling in the $15 range, or almost half of book value, after a year of lackluster earnings and several big write-offs had produced a net loss. The dividend yield was a respectable 4.5%. Therefore, G&W's stock looked like it didn't have much downside risk, but good upside potential if the company could get its act together.

In 1984 and 1985, Gulf & Western began one of the mose extensive transformations ever undertaken by an American company. It divested subsidiary companies, reduced debt, used liquid assets to repurchase shares, and implemented an aggressive acquisition program. Formerly a huge conglomerate, G&W became an entertainment, publishing, and financial services company. The restructuring was successful and investors recognized it. G&W's stock sold for nearly triple its book value by 1987.

Other total return investors who take the value-oriented approach to heart look at a company's breakup value—what it would be worth if it were dissolved and the operating units sold separately. Still others look for hidden assets on the balance sheet such as real estate and valuable franchise rights purchased years ago and carried at cost. These asset-oriented approaches can be useful when searching for anomalies in the normally efficient financial markets.

One successful money manager, Mario Gabelli, purchases stocks of companies whose private market value is more than its aggregate market price. The former is the price an informed corporate acquirer might be willing to pay to purchase company assets. This approach has worked well in an age of corporate restructuring, leveraged buy-outs, and takeovers. Gabelli has sold many of his holdings at very high premiums to market price.

Dividend Cuts and Omissions

In some cases, total return investors following the contrarian investment philosophy will invest in non-dividend paying stocks where the company once paid a dividend and then eliminated it as cash flows shrunk. These investors are betting on a dividend restoration to not only provide current yield but also to have a positive influence on the price of the shares they hold.

Dividend cuts usually occur with small capitalization companies; larger companies will do anything to maintain their dividends. It's the prestige factor of having an uninterrupted dividend payment history. Also, in contrast to smaller companies, they can better afford to dip into cash reserves to maintain dividends in a period of temporary adversity.

When the dividend is eventually restored, it signals a boost of confidence from management in the company's prospects. This normally has a beneficial impact on the price of the stock. Sometimes the shares begin to move on the plus side months before the actual dividend restoration occurs. If temporary negatives are out of the way and cash flow is improving, smart total return investors begin accumulating stock. They know the company directors will eventually restore the dividend.

An example of this occurred several years ago when a small electric and gas utility in the suburbs of Boston, Massachusetts went through a financial trauma. The comany was Fitchburg Gas and Electric and its shares traded on the American Stock Exchange. Fitchburg ran into trouble because of its small ownership interest in the ill-fated Seabrook, New Hampshire nuclear power plant. State politicians and regulators wanted Fitchburg to get out of the nuclear mess, so they withheld approval for the company's continued financing of the project. No bonds could be floated to pay for Fitchburg's participation in Seabrook.

Fitchburg's Board of Directors, realizing a cash crunch was on the way and wanting to impress upon the State government the importance of obtaining additional financing, voted to omit the dividend. This is a serious step for any public utility to take. Many shareholders depend on the dividend for income, having originally invested in the company for the high yield of its common stock. A number of them also lived in the service area and were doubly upset at the way the company was being treated.

Fitchburg's stock was selling for around $18 and it paid about $2 in dividends when the dividend cut was announced. Soon thereafter, the stock was trading at $9 with a number of very disappointed shareholders. This was the time for contrarians to bottom fish, even though pessimism was rampant.

Eventually the Seabrook investment was sold and Fitchburg Gas and Electric was allowed to issue new bonds. The stock began to move up as the company's finances improved. And guess what else happened? The dividend was partially restored to $1.52 in 1986.

After the share price recovered to $22, those total return investors who bought Fitchburg at $9 when everyone was singing the blues made heady profits of 145% on their investment in just two years. And if they continue to hold the stock, they'll receive a current yield of about 7% plus the chance for further dividend growth and capital appreciation. However, the dramatic returns of several years ago won't be repeated because this is a small electric utility with relatively slow growth prospects.

Timing Purchases of Out-of-Favor Stocks

In buying undervalued stocks, a margin of safety exists if the price of the stock has already fallen considerably. Contrarians prey on the tendency of market participants to exaggerate the significance of transitory negative events. Under the specter of gloom and doom, the share price often drops to unrealisticly low levels—below its intrinsic value. The margin of safety this creates is important to total return investors. It reduces risks. For although the price can certainly drop further, any more declines shouldn't be too great.

When is the right time to buy a fallen angel or otherwise depressed stock? This is a very difficult question to answer. Obviously you want to wait until practically all the bad news is out—the dividend has been omitted, the company president has been fired, or the strike has begun. This is the time of exteme pessimism when stockholders are dumping shares on the market as fast as they can unload them. When the price of the stock has come way down, wait for it to settle. After monitoring sideways price movements for a while, begin to accumulate your position.

Total return investors who bit the bullet and purchased shares of an out-of-favor soft drink company a few years ago are a happy lot. Back in 1982, Pepsico encountered problems on two fronts. Its subsidiary in Mexico was floundering because of the continual devaluation of the Mexican peso, which penalized the parent's earnings. In addition, several Pepsico executives were under the gun because of bribes to foreign governments. These negative developments pushed the stock below $35 a share, where the dividend yield was a solid 5%. Nevertheless, Pepsico was a well-managed company with a solid earnings history that had successfully diversified into the food industry.

Total return investors who recognized that Pepsico's corporate setbacks were only temporary were amply rewarded. Several years later, when earnings were on the upswing and the Mexican and foreign bribery problems were long forgotten, Pepsico's stock was selling at over $100 a share. Chalk up one more winner for the contrarians.

New Issue Bargain Hunting

Another fruitful area to look for total return bargains is in the new issue aftermarket. Companies go public when they've reached a certain size and have established a good five-year sales and earnings growth record. The owners need to raise capital for expansion or just want to cash in some of their chips and establish a liquid trading market for their holdings. After the initial public offering (IPO), something happens to the business fortunes of many of the new issue companies. They either can't handle the growth, fail at diversification, expand too rapidly, or competition becomes more intense.

One of several share price scenarios might occur: the stock is richly priced in the IPO, rises for a while, then falls back as earnings difficulties come to the fore. Or the company's stock is overpriced at the outset and immediately drops below the initial offering price. No buying support exists because underwriters are forbidden from issuing any research reports on the stock for at least 90 days after the offering.

Bargains can be had for those with the patience to look for fallen new issue shares anywhere from six to twelve months after their IPO. As with any depressed issue, a determination must be made that the problems are temporary and will eventually be rectified. There's no better feeling than paying a bargain-basement $10 a share for a stock that sold for $15 in the IPO, then watching it recover to the original offering price.

A case in point is Entertainment Publications, Inc., a midwest marketer of disount coupon books known as "two-fers." This company had an excellent earnings growth record (82% a year compounded in fiscal years 1980-1984) and was the biggest factor in the discount coupon industry when it went public at $12 a share in December, 1983. It was richly priced at 20 times trailing earnings, or twice the market multiple.

The Entertainment Publication stock went nowhere after the offering. Earnings trouble developed six months later and the stock price sunk to a tad above $8 a share. What happened was the company increased its penetration into new markets at a much quicker pace than anticipated. The business strategy was to pre-empt competition and establish the company as the only national distributor of discount coupon books. Higher corporate overhead to support the expansion, along with increased marketing costs, sent earnings down in fiscal 1985.

Total return investors willing to accept this negative earnings news as a temporary phenomenon profited handsomely. They knew current earnings were being sacrificed for future income and that the stock was a much better buy at $8 as opposed to the IPO price of $12. The market had truly discounted the discounter! In three years the stock rebounded from $8 to over

$20 a share as several brokerage houses started to recommend it as a long-term growth stock with a strong, established franchise.

Securities of Bankrupt Companies

Although buying shares of bankrupt companies must be considered the greatest expression of the contrarian investing philosophy, it isn't really total return investing in its purest sense. When a company goes into bankruptcy, not only are dividends suspended, so are principal and interest payments on debt. Therefore, shareholders receive no current return.

Contrarian investors sometimes do very well investing in bankrupt companies by reaping capital gains. Institutional investors often have to bail out of the stocks of bankrupt companies because they're not allowed to hold these securities in their clients' portfolios. (They also don't want anyone to know they once owned them.) This drives prices to artificially low levels as the securities markets become inefficient through fear and despair.

Several prominent American corporations have used the bankruptcy laws in an attempt to help them recover from huge judgments pending against them, notably A.H. Robins and Texaco. In both cases, sales and earnings prospects for their basic business were solid; the large lawsuits finally drove them to seek protection from creditors.

Robins is known for the Dalkon Shield claims of many female customers who bought this faulty interuterine birth control device. It filed for bankruptcy in August, 1985. Although the shares dropped from $20 to $5.50, smart investors realized the company had a strong line of products which included the well-known Robitussin cough medicine and Chap Stick lip balm. This made it an attractive acquisition candidate if the litigation claims could be worked out.

Sure enough, total return investors were rewarded for purchasing Robins' shares. A buy-out offer from a large drug and health-care products company, the Rorer Group, came in mid-1987. Robins' stock price recovered to the high $20's—more than quintupling within a short two years for some savvy investors.

Texaco faced a $10.3 billion judgment from Pennzoil after Texaco bought Getty Oil out from under Pennzoil, who thought it had an agreement to purchase part of Getty. In April 1987, Texaco filed for bankruptcy and the stock slid from $32 to $27 a share in one day, but recovered soon thereafter. At the time of filing, Texaco had a book value of $56 per share and paid a dividend of $3. Within several months, Texaco's stock had recovered into the mid $40s with talk of a compromise settlement with Pennzoil.

Total return profits from Texaco's bankruptcy weren't as great as with Robins, but the concept was the same. In both cases, company fundamentals were unusually strong. Robins had good product lines and Texaco had valuable oil and gas reserves. Total return investors willing to see beyond the immediate problems and who were able to recognize the value of each company's assets reaped excellent capital gains in a short period of time. Those with more patience will eventually see dividend distributions restored on Robins' and Texaco's shares.

Risks of Contrarian Investing

Several risks are involved with contrarian investing. The first is that the price of the out-of-favor stock never recovers. When no dividends are being paid, you earn absolutely nothing on the investment. You incur what is known as an opportunity cost, where you could have earned at least money market rates on your funds if they hadn't been invested in the stock. On the other hand, if dividends are paid as the share price languishes, the lack of capital gain is mitigated by the current income received while you wait.

The second risk is that the company's fundamentals continue to deteriorate. This leads to dividend cuts, dividend omission or, in the worst-case scenario, bankruptcy. Some companies whose shares appear undervalued on the surface may actually face above-average business problems that are chronic in nature. The stock price will probably erode further as hoped-for positive total returns vanish completely.

A third risk is more subtle. Out-of-favor stocks have the behavioral momentum of the market working against them. Institutions dump them from their portfolios and aren't about to buy back in. Wall Street analysts neglect them. Professional money managers are short-term oriented because of the tremendous performance pressures placed on them. They don't want to risk a long hold while waiting for a corporate turnaround. A lack of buying demand keeps prices low and any selling pressure drives them even lower.

Finally, it's also possible the negative investment psychology may never turn positive again. Wall Street has a long collective memory, especially when it's been burned once on a stock. Furthermore, if corporate management has a credibility problem with the Street, chances are the share price may languish for years.

An example of a stock that looked like a good contrarian bet but failed to pan out was that of Flow General Corporation. This New York Stock Exchange company supplies research and analyis to the Federal government along with biomedical products to the health industry. Back in 1982 it was a high-flying biotechnology outfit that took on a lot of debt to make a series of ill-fated acquisitions.

The stock sold as high as $45 a share before earnings came tumbling down in 1983. When the stock swooned to $10, the president was fired. New management came in (actually it was a former board chairman and the research director), but the troubles worsened. Laboratories were closed down by government officials, subsidiaries were sold off, and some of the onerous debt was paid off. The shares looked cheap at $7.50.

However, Flow General's stock drifted lower to $5, as earnings failed to recover. Losses were sustained in each year 1983 through 1986, with the prospects for 1987 appearing to be not much better. The stock is still selling at $6 a share. Anyone who bought on the way down has a paper loss. After a four-year wait, the outlook for eventual recovery is in serious doubt.

Importance of Cash Flow Analysis

How does one determine whether it's a good bet to invest in a growth stock or an out-of-favor one?. You have to look at the corporate financial statements. And one place to start with is the statement of changes in financial position. It appears after the income statement and balance sheet in a company's annual and quarterly reports. Using it, you can calculate cash flows and observe where funds are coming from and where they're going.

A statement of changes in financial position appearing in the 1987 Annual Report of National Medical Enterprises, Inc., a current out-of-favor company, is shown in Figure 2.

Figure 2

Consolidated Statements of Changes in Financial Position   National Medical Enterprises, Inc. and Subsidiaries

Years Ended May 31, 1987, 1986 and 1985

(dollar amounts are expressed in millions)	1987	1986	1985
Sources of working capital:			
Income from continuing operations	$ 140	$ 116	$ 144
Add: Depreciation and amortization	129	114	95
Deferred income taxes	43	20	56
Amortization of long-term debt discount	21	9	4
Restructuring costs	—	21	—
Other	11	31	12
Working capital provided by continuing operations	344	311	311
Income (loss) from discontinued operations	(77)	(22)	6
Add: Depreciation and amortization	15	24	17
Provision for loss on disposal	55	—	—
Other	—	15	—
Working capital provided by operations before extraordinary charge	337	328	334
Extraordinary charge, net of unamortized issue costs	—	7	—
Working capital provided by operations	337	335	334
Issuance or assumption of other long-term debt	277	175	348
Sale of property, plant and equipment	166	120	142
Sale of debentures and notes to public	—	216	292
Reissuance of treasury stock for stock benefit plans	14	—	—
Other	24	59	40
Total sources	818	905	1,156
Dispositions of working capital:			
Additions to property, plant and equipment:			
Purchased businesses	59	198	161
Other	322	302	281
Reductions of long-term debt	139	181	364
Purchases of treasury stock	128	—	—
Redemption of debentures	45	123	—
Cash dividends	44	43	36
Additions to intangible assets	24	23	103
Increase in notes receivable, investments and other assets	5	124	81
Total dispositions	766	994	1,026
Increase (decrease) in working capital	$ 52	$ (89)	$ 130
Increase (decrease) in working capital by element:			
Cash and short-term investments	$ (19)	$ (6)	$ (4)
Accounts and notes receivable	18	69	189
Other current assets	39	9	11
Current portion of long-term debt	(34)	(1)	(4)
Short-term borrowings and notes	7	(75)	18
Accounts payable and other current liabilities	(20)	(71)	(26)
Income taxes payable	61	(14)	(54)
Increase (decrease) in working capital	$ 52	$ (89)	$ 130

See accompanying notes to consolidated financial statements.

Total return investors should learn the ABC's of cash flow analysis because this is important to a corporation's ability (or inability) to maintain the dividend in the case of fallen angel stocks and increase it in the case of growth stocks. With recent tax law changes lowering corporate tax rates, many companies will be looking to increase shareholder dividends; those with strong cash flows can do it easier and quicker.

Cash flow is simply a company's reported after-tax earnings and non-cash expenditures added together. These latter items often include depreciation, amortization, deferred taxes, write-offs of investments, and other items where no actual cash outlay is involved. The depreciation item is usually the largest non-cash charge.

The amount of cash flow generated per share indicates the state of a company's health and its ability to pay dividends on its common stock, as well as increase them. As explained earlier, this helps determine its stock price based on the discounted future stream of dividends theory.

Many industries with heavy depreciation charges will have cash flows which are double or triple per share earnings. However, for some industries the depreciation item must be considered like a cash charge because plant and equipment are actually wasting due to wear and tear and obsolescence. These fixed assets must eventually be replaced using real cash.

For other businesses, the depreciation is truly a non-cash charge. Prime examples are the cable TV and broadcasting industries, where property, equipment, and franchise costs may be depreciated over five years. The actual wear and tear on the system is a lot less. In fact, analysts value cable TV systems on a multiple of cash flow, rather than on reported earnings. The same goes for the broadcasting industry, where operating licenses are bought and depreciated, yet no actual obsolescence takes place.

A well-known contrarian investor and author, David Dreman, researched cash flow data on 750 of the largest public companies from 1963 to 1985. He separated them into five equal groups ranking them each year according to their ratio of cash flow to market price. The returns were measured annually. Over the entire 22 year period, the stocks with the highest price to cash flow ratio had a 10.7% toal return annually, while those with the lowest ratio returned 20.1%. This is strong evidence of the influence of cash flows on the future price of a stock.

In summary, what do you look for when considering the purchase of total return stocks? Growth stock companies should have hiked their common dividend at least once a year for each of the past 10 years. There must be a good reason why no increase was forthcoming in any particular year.

Look for growth stocks where dividend increases average at least 10% a year. At a minimum, the dividend should double every 10 years. If possible, a growth stock should have a current yield higher than that of the S&P 500 Stock Index. Remember, on a historical basis dividend income has made up 60% to 65% of the total returns realized from common stock investments. That's a good reason to emphasize yield over the longer term.

For value-oriented total return investors, ideal stocks to consider are those which sell for less than book value, are priced at a discount to the stock market's average price-earnings multiple, and have a dividend yield 50% higher than the market yield. Also look for stocks that have retreated at least 50% from their highs. With a little hard work on your part or through your financial advisor, these stocks can be found. The easy task will be reaping the total return rewards.

The next chapter will explain how a certain group of corporate bonds can be used as total return investments.

Chapter 5

Total Return Corporate Bonds

Investing in corporate bonds for total return may seem at first blush to be an impossible task. Current returns from bonds are fixed. Their prices fluctuate mostly in response to changes in interest rates. Aggressive investors view them as rather boring. But astute investors can achieve above-average total returns from certain bonds if they do their homework, look for value, and are willing to exercise a little patience. You won't hit home runs with bonds, but by looking for inefficiencies in the market, you can hit a lot of singles, doubles, and an occasional triple with them.

Playing the interest rate game with bonds in order to realize capital gains will not be discussed in this book. To make money with this approach, you have to be right twice—once when you buy the bonds and once when you sell. If you're right and buy bonds before interest rates go down, you have a good chance at garnering a capital gain in addition to the interest income received. However, if you guess wrong and rates go up, then in all likelihood you'll end up with a negative total return.

The corporate bonds appropriate for total return investors are discount straight bonds. You may ask, What exactly are these? "Straight" bonds are the pure vanilla variety—they don't have equity conversion or other unusual features associated with them. "Discount" bonds trade considerably below par value ($1,000) and usually have less than investment quality ratings (B or lower) by the major rating services. Therefore, a "discount straight bond" is a standard bond that trades below par for one reason or other.

Total return investors purchase discount corporate bonds with the hope the marketplace will recognize an improvement in the issuer's financial health which is reflected in a higher-quality bond. If an upgrading eventually occurs, the value of the bond should increase regardless of small changes in the level of interest rates. The total return bondholder realizes capital appreciation, as well as above-average yield in the form of high interest payments.

For instance, a discount bond selling for 75% of par value, or $750, may be bid up in price to $800 if the public perceives the risk of default has been reduced. Assume this happens in a year's time to a 10-year bond with a coupon rate of 9%. The total return will be 18.7%, comprised of 12% in current yield plus 6.7% of capital appreciation. Not bad for a one year investment.

Lending further credence to the total return concept of investing in discount bonds are the many studies which show that a well-diversified portfolio of low-quality bonds held until maturity will give a higher net yield, after all losses are considered, than a portfolio of high-quality bonds. These bonds must be held through periods of good economic times and difficult times. Unfortunately, not everyone has the resources or right temperment to pursue this investment strategy.

Bond Market Inefficiencies

Total return bond investors realize that inefficiencies exist in the bond market and they hope to take advantage of them. Institutional investors—pension funds and insurance companies—prefer to purchase bonds when they're offered as new issues because they can buy in size without disrupting markets. They place their orders with the underwriting group and make a final purchase decision when the price and other terms are announced.

If the bonds drop in value after the offering because of the issuing company's poor financial performance, institutions often bail out. They don't want the paper of weak companies showing up on their books at review time. The additional selling pressure depresses prices further to unrealisticly low levels. These fallen angel bonds are avoided in the secondary market by both institutions and individuals. Through searching for bargains in this imperfect market, total return investors can reap substantial profits.

Here's an example of how bond market inefficiencies can inure to the benefit of the total return investor. The Chrysler Corporation had A-rated bonds back in the mid-1970s. Then the auto company sustained losses of $1 billion in 1979 and $1.7 billion in 1980. Institutions over-reacted and began dumping Chrysler debt. The 8% sinking fund debentures due 1998 nosedived to as low as $280 in 1981 for a current yield of 28.7%. By 1982, the rating on the bonds had dropped all the way down to CC as the company's financial condition deteriorated to the point here it faced the grim prospect of filing for Chapter 11 bankruptcy.

As Chrysler's finances improved under the leadership of Lee Iaccoca—with a bit of help from a government loan and the end of the deep recession of the early Reagan presidency—the bonds recovered to $900 and the rating improved to BBB. Astute investors willing to bet on the recovery of America's third largest automobile manufacturer purchased Chrysler bonds in the midst of doom and gloom. They reaped profits of 220% in six years from a normally unglamorous, straight bond investment.

Other major American companies in addition to Chrysler have succumbed to the category of "fallen angels." These include Penn Central, Montgomery Ward, Ford Motor Company, and International Harvester. They were mature companies in mature industries, weakened by internal operating problems, external competition, or declining markets. One way or another, they've all recovered from their problems.

By understanding the dynamics of management change, cost cutting, restructuring, and other factors necessary for a company to turn its fortunes around, the total return investor can buy, at a significant discount to par value, bonds that once again could become quite valuable. You can put the inefficiencies of the bond market to work for your benefit.

Take the case of International Harvester, now known as Navistar. It was severely crippled by the depression in the farm belt in the early 1980s. At that time, its 6.25% sinking fund debentures of 1998 sold as low as $210 apiece. It seemed no one wanted to own Harvester bonds.

Five years later, after Harvester restructured itself from a farm equipment maker to a truck manufacturer and changed its name, the bonds increased in value to $700 as the company's financial prospects improved considerably. Patient total return investors who bought at the bottom were well-rewarded with a 230% profit plus annual yields in the double-digit range.

Bond Prices and Quotes

For persons unfamiliar with the concept, or those who need to have their memories refreshed, each bond customarily has a par value of $1,000. All quotations appearing in the financial pages of the newspaper are expressed as percentages of value. Therefore, a $1,000 bond listed in the newspaper at 85 is worth 85% of $1,000 or $850. It sells at a discount to par. One trading at 107 is worth $1,070 and sells at a premium to par.

Only a small fraction of corporate bond issues are listed on the New York Stock Exchange and the American Stock Exchange (they actually appear in the bond sections). You can find daily price information on exchange-listed bonds in the major newspapers such as the *Wall Street Journal* and the *New York Times*.

A majority of corporate bonds sell in the over-the-counter market. The large issues of $100 million or more usually have good liquidity. But expect to pay a slight premium for small orders because bonds most often trade in lot sizes of at least $100,000. In addition, it's hard to follow price movements for the OTC bonds unless you subscribe to the pink sheets or sign up with a stock market quote service. With the latter, you can receive real-time market price quotes on a personal computer via a modem and telephone lines.

Bond Ratings

As all serious investors know, the major security rating services, Moody's Investor Services, Inc. and Standard & Poor's Corporation, classify bonds into several quality rating categories. Basically, it's their staffs' current assessment of the creditworthiness of the obligor with respect to a specific debt issue. The bond issuing company (called the issuer) pays the services to provide the ratings. Usually the two services assign the same rating to each issue; if they don't, then the ratings are very close.

Moody's and Standard & Poor's rely on the same publicly available financial information to conduct their credit analyses; they don't perform independent audits on the companies reviewed. No inside information is dispensed. The rating services have large staffs of analysts who pour over company and industry data to come up with their credit rating recommendations.

Standard & Poor's AAA and Moody's Aaa designation (notice the similarity of the two) are the highest ratings bestowed upon a debt issue. An AAA-rated company is characterized by an extremely strong capacity to pay its debt obligations. It should be pointed out that very few corporate bonds receive the top ratings—less than 25—and only 800 qualify as investment grade (A or better). The full range of quality ratings by each service is shown in Table 1.

Table 1: Bond Rating System

S&P	Moody's	
AAA	Aaa	Investment Grade - Capacity to pay principal and interest extremely strong
AA	Aa	Investment Grade - Capacity very strong
A	A	Investment Grade - Capacity strong, but somewhat susceptible to economic downswings
BB	Baa	Medium Investment Grade - Adequate capacity, but adverse economic conditions or changing circumstances are more likely to lead to weakened capacity to pay interest and repay principal
BB	Ba	Somewhat Speculative
B	B	Speculative
CCC	Caa	Outright Speculative
CC	Ca	Highly Speculative
C	C	Highest Degree of Speculation
D	D	Default - Payments in arrears
NR	UNR	Unrated - No rating requested or insufficient information available

In recent years the rating services have gone one step further and assigned pluses (+) and minuses (-) to corporate bonds they rate to provide a more exact indication of how the issues stand within the major rating categories. For example, a BBB+ rating is a strong BBB, while an A- is a weak A. It's similar to school grades received on coursework. And like a teacher's grading of a student essay, developing the proper rating is just as much an art as it is a science.

While by no means foolproof, the ratings Moody's and S&P assign bonds are a fairly good indication of the default rate or the inability of the issuing company to pay interest and principal on a timely basis. Higher quality bonds have lower default rates; conversely, lower quality bonds have higher default rates. In a study conducted a number of years ago, the default rate of A-rated bonds was more than double the default rate on AAA and AA bonds, while the default rate on BBB bonds was triple that of the two highest-rated categories.

Since World War II, less than 5% of all B-rated bonds have defaulted. A study done of a more recent period showed defaults of BB or lower-rated bonds averaged only 1.5% a year. While this percent sounds low, it's actually 20 times the rate for all corporate debt during the same period. Even in bankruptcy-ridden 1982, only $830 million of $340 billion, or .2% of all corporate debt, went into default.

Not only are Moody's and Standard & Poor's staffs continuously rating debt issues, but the market place also grades their quality through the interaction of the forces of supply and demand. These price movements come more quickly than rating changes. In fact, the agencies often amend their ratings long after the market price of the bonds has adjusted to the new financial condition of the issuing company. It takes agency analysts time to review the latest data, make appropriate recommendations, and publish new ratings. Both agencies are quite sensitive to arguments that they're more reactive than proactive in changing their ratings.

In an attempt to mollify criticism, Standard & Poor's and Moody's, through a system called Creditwatch, periodically announce which companies will undergo review for potential change in ratings based on a special event such as a merger, stock repurchase, action by a regulatory agency, or other major development. The investment world is put on notice for upgradings and downgradings. Each agency gives itself 90 days to make a rating decision.

Yield Spread

The price quotations and yields in the bond market are evidence of how investors rate various fixed-income securities. This creates a yield spread, or the difference in yields on two bonds with the same maturity. A bond that is perceived to be of higher quality will sell at a lower yield than one which investors feel carries more risk.

Historically, in periods of prosperity the yield spread between AAA and BBB bonds stays in a range of 50-75 basis points (100 basis points equals 1%, so this difference is the same as 1/2% to 3/4% of yield). During recessions, the yield spread between AAA and BBB bonds increases to several hundred basis points (2% to 3%) because greater uncertainty exists regarding the safety of lower-rated bonds. (This also happens to be the best time to buy bonds for capital gains.) With economic recovery on the way, investors anticipating better business conditions, and companies with lower-rated bonds finding it easier to pay debts, the yield spread compresses back to 50-75 basis points.

The yield spread during the business cycle is illustrated in Figure 1.

Figure 1: Current Yield Spread Between High and Low-Rated Bonds

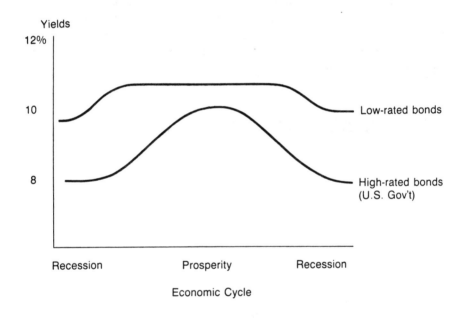

In June, 1982, with a recession in full swing, the spread between high-yield bonds and U.S. Government bonds was six percentage points. In less than three months, it dropped to 3.5%. The level of interest rates dropped dramatically, corporate liquidity improved, and the economy appeared well on the road to recovery.

Investors receive anywhere from two to five percentage points greater yield from lower-rated bond issues than from high-grade corporates. This is the yield premium earned for taking on more risk. If the total return investor does his homework, he'll find many of these high-yielding bonds to be reasonably safe.

Yields to Maturity

All corporate bonds must be paid off at maturity at par value or $1,000 per bond. Those selling at discounts to par have an element of built-in capital appreciation, wherein over the life of the bond the price rises inexorably toward $1,000, all other things remaining the same. In other words, a bond selling for $750 and maturing in ten years will gain $250 in value along the way. Table 2 shows the theoretical increase in value of the bond as it reaches maturity. Naturally, this assumes the company will have adequate funds to make the required sinking fund payments and any remaining principal payments at maturity.

Table 2: Increase In Bond Value

Years to Maturity	Value	Increase in Value
10	$750.00	–
9	762.50	12.50
8	777.50	15.00
7	795.00	17.50
6	815.00	20.00
5	835.00	20.00
4	860.00	25.00
3	887.50	27.50
2	920.00	32.50
1	957.50	37.50
0	1000.00	42.50

Calculating yields to maturity on discount bonds is important. The yield to maturity for 10-year bond with a 9% coupon rate priced at $750 works out to 13.7%. This is arrived at by taking the annual interest payment of

$90 and adding the $12.50 theoretical increase in value from the tenth to the ninth year to maturity (from Table 2) and then dividing by $750. Several companies publish Bond Yield Tables, which are handy reference for quickly calculating yields to maturity.

As can be seen from Table 2, the closer the bond gets to maturity the more it rises in value. However, on a percentage basis, the movement upwards is not as pronounced. From year 9 to year 8 the increase is almost 2%, whereas from year 2 to 1 the increase is 4.1%.

Based on this analysis, one might rationalize that it's better to wait until a discount bond nears maturity before buying in order to realize the greatest percentage price appreciation. However, this isn't a good rule of thumb to use because so many other factors determine the price of the bond during the course of its life, including interest rate levels, sinking fund activity, the issuer's financial prospects, and bond scarcity.

Effect of Sinking Fund Payments

Most bond issues are set up so that the issuer is obligated to make sinking fund payments to retire most of the issue prior to maturity. The company must pay the bond trustee the equivalent of 5% or 10% of the issue each year, depending on the length of maturity. This is usually set at 5% annually for a 25-year bond and 10% for a 15-year bond.

Bonds purchased by the issuer in the secondary market may be substituted for cash payments to the trustee. If cash is eventually paid, the trustee uses it to redeem the bonds by lottery. This sinking fund procedure leaves little or no balloon payment for the issuing company in the year the bonds mature.

It's important to know when these sinking fund payments begin and their annual amounts. The payments may put a strain on a weak company's cash flow. Table 3 shows the effect of the sinking fund payments on the amount of bonds outstanding during the life of a 15-year, $25 million issue, where payments start in the sixth year at 10% per year:

When the bonds are selling at a discount to par, the issuing company usually buys enough in the secondary market to satisfy the sinking fund payment rather than have the trustee redeem them at par plus a premium. This saves money. Corporate activity of this nature also provides important price support for the bonds and a chance for total return investors to liquidate holdings in an orderly way.

Sometimes the bonds are selling above par or the issuer can't buy enough of them in the secondary market to satisfy the sinking fund requirement. In these situations, the issuer will have the trustee redeem them by lottery, paying a premium based on the coupon rate. For a bond with a 10% coupon, the first redemption will be at $1,100. The premium scales down each year to where it reaches zero when the bond matures. It's an added expense necessary to compensate the bondholder for an early redemption.

Table 3: Sinking Fund Payments Retire Debt

End of Year	Sinking Fund Payment	Balance of Issue
1	0	$25,000,000
2	0	25,000,000
3	0	25,000,000
4	0	25,000,000
5	0	25,000,000
6	$2,500,000	22,500,000
7	2,500,000	20,000,000
8	2,500,000	17,500,000
9	2,500,000	15,000,000
10	2,500,000	12,500,000
11	2,500,000	10,000,000
12	2,500,000	7,500,000
13	2,500,000	5,000,000
14	2,500,000	2,500,000
15	2,500,000	0

Bond Calls

It should be pointed out that limits exist as to the total returns that can be generated from straight bond investing. Bond prices do not go up forever. Once the price of a non-convertible discount bond hits par, further upward movement is hard to come by unless interest rates drop significantly. Yet when this happens, the financially stronger issuer may be able to replace the bonds with less expensive debt.

The issuing company can refund the debt if it has what are known as call provisions in the bond indenture. This document is like a contract between the issuer and its bondholders. A call privilege gives the company the right to redeem all or part of the bonds after a certain period of time, usually five years from the date of issue. If the company calls the bonds, the owners receive par plus a small premium (a percentage over par) which, when added together, is often less than the market price of the bonds. This threat of a premature redemption is obviously a negative for total return investors whose bonds have gone way above par.

By sticking to the ownership of discount bonds, you're well-protected from early calls as long as the bonds remain below par. Only in very unusual cases would a company call these bonds and pay a premium. And a company won't refinance its debt unless it has the financial strength to float new bonds.

When buying discount bonds, it's always best to look for bonds with call protection of at least 4 to 5 years. During this period, the company cannot call the bonds for any reason whatsoever. You'll pay a slight market premium for them, but it may be worth it if the company's fortunes change and the bonds reach par. You'll be able to lock in the high coupon rate for quite some time.

Even when the issue is called, the total return investor comes out a winner because he usually receives a premium for bonds he bought at a discount. Instead of $1000, he receives $1050 for a bond which cost only $800. It's hard to complain when that happens.

Financial Statement Analysis

What does one look for in a company's income statement and balance sheet to analyze the prospects for a total return bond? With the income statement, the concern is with the size of all interest payments compared to pre-tax earnings. Since interest costs are tax deductible, the key figure to look at is earnings before taxes and non-recurring charges. As a budding bond analyst, you want to know the amount of earnings available to cover debt payments. Expressed in ratio form, by how many times are the interest payments covered by earnings and, most importantly, is this ratio improving or worsening?

Here's an example of Company ABC's interest coverage:

Interest Coverage for ABC Company

Earnings before interest and taxes(1)	$100,000,000
Interest expense (2)	20,000,000
Earnings before taxes	80,000,000
Taxes at 34%	27,000,000
Net income	$ 53,000,000
Coverage: (1) divided by (2)	5.0

This is a financially strong company, one with the equivalent of an A or AA Standard & Poor's rating. Company ABC's interest coverage of five times is excellent. On the other hand, the bonds of Company XYZ with the following financials would be much lower-rated and would be typical of bond investments that total return investors would consider for their portfolios:

Interest Coverage for XYZ Company

Earnings before interest (1)	$ 3,000,000
Interest expense (2)	2,000,000
Earnings before taxes	1,000,000
Taxes at 34%	340,000
Net income	$ 660,000
Coverage: (1) divided by (2)	1.5

In the case of Company XYZ, the interest payment coverage has dropped to 1.5. The company has only $1.50 of earnings to pay each dollar of interest expense. This represents a high degree of operating leverage and greater risk of an inability to meet interest payments under adverse business conditions.

As for examining the balance sheet, the total return bond investor is concerned with the magnitude of all corporate debt and its relationship to stockholder equity. A popular measure is the debt-equity ratio, shown below for a hypothetical company:

Debt and Equity Portions of Balance Sheet

Senior debt	$100,000,000
Subordinated debt	50,000,000
Total debt	$150,000,000
Capital stock	25,000,000
Retained earnings	125,000,000
Stockholder equity	$150,000,000

In this example, the debt/equity ratio is 1:1, with debt of $150 million and equity of $150 million. This appears to be a fairly well-leveraged company. Ratios of 1:3 or greater ($50 million debt and $150 million equity) indicate much less leverage and better asset and earnings support for the debt as long as the company is generating a good return on equity.

You'll also want to know how much debt is coming due in the next several years. This can be gleaned by looking at the footnotes to the financial statements in the issuer's annual report where there is a schedule of future debt payments. Whether or not these repayments can be handled easily depends on the amount of cash generated from operations. The more discretionary cash, the merrier.

Traditional corporate bond investing is often viewed as a negative art. The analyst is always looking for bad things that can affect a bond's price and rating. Institutional investors search for early warning signals that could negatively impact the bond price. They want to be able to bail out ahead of any unfavorable news.

Total return investors, on the other hand, practice the positive art of bond investing. They look at downtrodden bonds and figure out how their lot might be improved. Those persons who invest in discount bonds have an advantage—the negatives are already out on the table. The total return investor's job is the find out what they are, and gaze into the chrystal ball to ascertain when they'll likely take a turn for the better and therefore have a positive effect on the bond price.

With lower-rated bonds, standard interest coverage figures and balance sheet ratio measures will not necessarily apply. The investor has to examine trends in cash flow, the timing of mandatory debt payments, and the prospects for a turnaround in corporate earnings. He also has to look at the cyclicality of the industry in which the issuing company operates.

The concept of cash flow was discussed in the previous chapter on total return stocks. To repeat briefly, cash flow includes non-cash charges such as depreciation, depletion allowances, and amortization expenses in addition to net income. This represents the total amount of cash generated from operations that can be used for dividends, debt servicing, plant and equipment expansions, or additions to working capital. It's one of the best measures of a company's actual strength or weakness.

A more sophisticated measure of corporate financial strength is the availability of "free cash flow." This is cash generated from operations less that needed for debt servicing (making both interest and principal payments) and capital expenditures. The free cash flow is discretionary cash available for a variety of non-mandatory purposes such as dividends on common stock, acquisitions, or stock repurchases.

The astute total return bond investor will also want to look at each of the company's operating businesses—its divisions and subsidiaries—to determine if they are attractive sale candidates and can be divested should the company's finances deteriorate further. This gives another layer of protection to bondholders. Asset sales can be used to tide a company over or pay back debt. Lower debt service requirements may actually strengthen the value of the remaining bonds.

Maybe a company with discount bonds has large net operating loss carryfowards that another company can use to reduce its tax burden. This transforms a financially-weak company into an attractive acquisition candidate. Or the issuer may have long-term leases at low rents that make the assignment of them a very valuable asset. No matter where the hidden value is located, successful total return bond investors are the ones who can recognize it as added insurance for the discount bonds if the company's financial condition worsens.

Selecting Discount Bonds

How do you identify likely bond candidates to achieve above-average total returns? You need to focus on BB, B, and possibly some CCC-rated discount corporate bonds—those in the middle categories, several notches below investment grade. These bonds have the best opportunity to increase in price should the issuer's fundamentals improve. Although the issuing companies are not financially strong, their bonds are less likely to go into default than the lowest-rated bonds of the weakest companies.

Unrated bonds also merit attention, even though you'll have to do your own credit analysis to determine what their ratings ought to be. Market yields on these bonds help in this determination. It's an indication of how other investors perceive the credit quality of the issuer.

Bonds selling between 80% and 90% of par value may be the best buy, particularly if you can find ones with maturities of less than 10 years. Shorter maturities mean less price volatility when interest rates move up and down, and a quicker time to payoff at par value. Short and medium-term discount bonds have a built-in booster which drives the price up to par as maturity time approaches.

If the credit rating for a company improves from a B to a BB or even BBB, the price of a straight bond should increase regardless of general movements in interest rates. For example, take a 10-year, B-rated bond with an 11% coupon that trades at $915 for a current yield a shade above 12%. Assume that over the course of a year the fundamental outlook for the company improves to such an extent that the bond now trades as if it carried a BB rating. Its price might rise to $1,000, generating an $85 profit equal to a 9.3% appreciation.

The chances of the price of the 10-year 11% coupon bond moving much above par are not as great as achieving the gains already realized. A hefty drop in interest rates is needed. As they say in the world of finance, the "easy money was made." But annual total returns of 21.3% on a 11% bond are quite respectible.

Another way to locate good discount bonds is through prospecting for common stock investments. If you discover an interesting, out-of-favor or neglected company, find out whether it also has any debt issues that look attractive. Usually the bonds will be selling at a discount to par value and carry low ratings from Moody's and Standard & Poor's. Perhaps no common dividends are being paid, but the company appears ripe for a turn-around. If the fundamentals for the company improve, then the bonds should have room for an upward price movement.

Investment opportunities in discount bonds present themselves when negative corporate news is announced, such as lower earnings, plant shutdowns, or the death of a key official. In the case of Chrysler, the news was in the national press with extensive TV and magazine coverage.

Don't back away in the face of temporary adversity when timid investors are selling out in a panic. Their mistake may mean your profit. Many times the picture will right itself in a matter of months and your patience will pay off. New management, a windfall from the sale of corporate assets, or a merger can drive the price of the bonds right back up again.

At other times, a company with discount bonds outstanding is experiencing a cyclical downturn or is in an industry that's unpopular with investors. The total return investor is attracted to this opportunity because he feels that the current income benefits from the ownership of discount bonds are excellent, while the long-term capital appreciation prospects are even better.

Care must be taken to monitor the company's prospects, detect any further deterioration in fundamentals, and sell before a major financial crisis develops. Absent any problems, the debt should be paid off at face value at maturity, making for a happy total return investor.

Bonds of Bankrupt Companies

One interesting facet of corporate bond investing is the purchase of defaulted debt securities of bankrupt companies. These deep-discount bonds generate the highest returns but also entail the most risk. The problem here is that it's often anyone's guess as to how each class of creditors and holders of equity securities will fare in final plan negotiations. Sometimes the creditors get a package of reconstituted debt and equity. Or they exchange their bonds for equity, weakening their claims on the assets and earning power of the reorganized company.

An additional problem is that during bankruptcy all interest payments on debt are suspended—total return investors get no current income while they wait. Although large profits can be made by patient investors, investing in debt securities of bankrupt companies is usually best left to the professionals who have the time and skills to analyze the ramifications of various reorganization scenarios.

The staff of investment advisors at Heine Securities have been very successful in this regard. They manage the Mutual Share group of no-load funds and have the experience to understand all the ins and outs of this type of investing. Their excellent performance record with the Mutual Qualified Income Fund and the Mutual Shares Corporation Fund is testimony to that fact.

High-Yield Junk Bonds

No discussion of investing in total return corporate bonds would be complete without a review of the popular junk bond phenomenon. These securities are also known as high-yield bonds, non-investment grade bonds, or bonds rated BB or lower. Their investment merits and demerits are widely debated in financial circles.

Very few companies qualify for investment grade ratings by Moody's and Standard & Poor's. In fact, less than 800 companies have ratings of BBB or better. The other 20,000 American companies with sales in excess of $25 million cannot obtain investment grade ratings because of their small size, limited capital structure, or lack of earnings history. Yet many of them are highly profitable companies with good growth prospects.

In the old days, these less fortunate companies raised capital by structuring private placements with insurance companies, pension funds, and other institutional investors. They paid not only a high interest rate on their borrowings, but had to sweeten the deals by giving up part of company ownership through equity kickers such as warrants or options to buy stock. These lesser-known, lower-rated companies could not tap the public securities markets to sell straight debt issues.

With the high-yield bond market coming of age in the mid 1980s, these small growth companies now have the public market to turn to for debt financing needs. The trade-off is somewhat higher borrowing costs in exchange for no equity give-ups. This is an important means for financing the growth of these companies without diluting management's shareholdings.

Thanks to the junk bond market, total return investors now have the opportunity to chose from a wider variety of lower-quality issues. For these investors, the rewards can be high if the bonds increase in value due to an upgrading of the credit rating as the issuing company matures and its debt servicing capacity strengthens.

Back in 1979, Golden Nugget, a casino operator in Nevada and Atlantic City, was a B-rated company with earnings of only $4 million. It issued 12.25% sinking fund debentures due in 1994. The bonds fell in price to $720 when interest rates rose. By July, 1983, the rating was upgraded to BB as the company's earnings soared to $40 million. The improving trend of earnings, coupled with lower interest rates, caused the price of the bonds to be bid up to $1,100 in four years time. Investors who bought Golden Nugget debt back in 1979 hit the jackpot with their straight bond investment.

One should ask the obvious question, Why buy junk bonds rather than the stock if the company's fortunes turn around? Aren't the potential returns greater through stock ownership? Yes, but the risks are greater than owning the bonds. In all likelihood no common stock dividends are being paid because of the company's poor financial condition. The investor is speculating solely on capital appreciation of the stock for his returns. If a turnaround doesn't occur, the investor receives absolutely no return on the stock investment; he suffers the opportunity cost of having made an investment with a zero return, whereas he could have earned something by parking funds in a money market account.

The total return discount bond investor, on the other hand, receives current income even if the company's prospects remain the same. He stands to gain part of his total return as interest payments and suffers only if the company's finances deteriorate further. In other words, he gets paid for waiting for the turnaround. And don't forget, the total return investor is in a more secure position than the common shareholder.

Junk bonds have also grown in popularity as a vehicle for raising funds for mergers and acquisitions, leveraged buyouts, and other similar corporate ventures. Basically, these bonds are of the high-coupon variety, often issued at discount and subordinated to other debt. The issuing company has a very leveraged balance sheet with loads of debt relative to equity. Hopefully, it has the earning power to make the principal and interest payments when they come due.

Total return investors may want to buy some of these high-yield issues, but the returns will probably be slower coming than by sticking with less leveraged situations. The reason is that it usually takes leveraged buyout companies a number of years to pay down the debt from operating cash flow. With high leverage, a downturn in company fortunes could imperil the debt payments. In addition, these bonds are not issued to finance growth, expansion and innovation, but to finance mergers, corporate restructuring, and ownership changes.

In summary, the total return corporate bond investor should concentrate on discount bonds selling in the $800 to $900 range for greater potential returns with lesser risk. In most cases, the issuer will be a small growth company or a financially weak larger company. Capital appreciation comes from an upgrading in the issuer's credit rating. The risk of loss from any one bond purchase can be reduced through proper portfolio diversification.

The next chapter deals with what are often referred to as "classic" total return securities—convertible bonds and preferred stocks.

Chapter 6

Total Return Convertible Securities

The quintessential total return securities are convertible bonds and preferred stocks. They provide total return investors with a relatively high current income and good capital appreciation potential. Convertibles are popular with investors who are willing to take less in yield than from a straight bond or preferred stock (but more current yield than from the common stock) in return for a chance at capital gains.

Total returns generated from a convertible security are very dependent on the action of the underlying stock. If the price of the stock goes up, the convert price will follow, but at a slower pace. Studies have shown that on average, convertible securities participate in 65% to 75% of the rise in the price of their "sister" common stocks.

Convertible holders receive the additional benefit of price protection on the downside, for there's a floor below which convertibles will not trade— its value as a straight bond or preferred stock. On average, convertibles participate in only 50% of the decline of the underlying common stock. Meanwhile, they command a yield advantage of between 3% and 10% over the common. These features make convertible securities very attractive to total return investors who want to limit risk and maximize returns. Table 1 shows just how this works.

In Table 1, the convertible security participates in much of the growth potential of the common stock, as evidenced by its upward price action of 35% in response to the stock price rise of 50%; yet there's much less risk in the event the common price drops (-25% versus -50%). And its yield advantage of 4% is an important factor when the price of the common remains stable. Overall, the convert represents a very favorable risk/reward scenario for the total return investor.

Table 1: Total Returns for Convertible Bond versus Common Stock

Common Stock

Price Change	+50%	+0%	−50%
Yield	+ 4	+4	+ 4
Total Return	+54	+4	−46

Convertible Security

Price Change	+35	0	−25
Yield	+ 8	+8	+ 8
Total Return	+43	+8	−17

Convertible bonds are a hybrid between a stock and a bond. Because of their fixed-income and maturity date features, they're technically classified as debt securities. The converts are usually subordinate to other debt when it comes to payment of interest and principal and any claims on company assets. If the issuing company prospers and the stock and the convertible bond do well, in all probablility the bond will be converted into common shares and become part of the company's equity.

Availability of Convertible Bonds

Convertibles are no longer issued by marginal companies hoping to raise funds at a cheap rate; even Big Blue, IBM, has a $1.25 billion convertible bond issue outstanding, the 7.875% due in the year 2004. And Ma Bell (AT&T), before it was broken up into the Baby Bells, used the convertible medium to raise capital. Other blue chip companies including Xerox, Chase Manhattan Corp., H. J. Heinz, J. P. Morgan, Pfizer, and Westinghouse Electric have sold convertible bonds to the public.

The level of convertible debt financing by American companies has increased dramatically over the last few years, making more merchandise available for the total return investor. This is illustrated in Table 2.

Table 2: New Issues of Corporate Convertible Debt

1982	$3.2 billion
1983	6.1 "
1984	4.1 "
1985	10.3 "
1986	11.0 "

Source: *Investment Dealers Digest.*

Like other bonds, convertibles are sold in denominations of $1,000 and have semi-annual interest payments. Over 650 of them appear in the Standard & Poor's Bond Guide. At least 150 trade on the New York Stock Exchange with another 20 or so listed on the American Exchange. With a fairly active convertible bond market, total return investors shouldn't be too worried about wide spreads between bid and asked prices as long as they stick to buying and selling bonds from the larger issues of $25 million and up.

Pricing of Convertibles

The conversion price of the bond is fixed until maturity. The only time an adjustment is made occurs when the common shareholders receive a stock split, stock dividend, or some other dilutive action is taken. For example, if a company had a bond that was convertible into 50 shares of common and the underlying stock was split two-for-one, then the stock conversion rate would be adjusted from 50 shares to 100 shares. Conversely, the conversion price is adjusted from $20 down to $10. This is the only equitable way for bondholders to protect their interests.

How are convertible bonds priced in the marketplace? The first part of the answer comes from examining the relationship between the price of the convert and the conversion value of the bond. Take a bond that's convertible into underlying stock at $25 a share, or 40 shares of stock for each $1,000 bond. Table 3 shows what happens to the bond value when the price of the stock moves up, assuming the bond has no coupon rate or conversion premium.

Table 3: Conversion Value of Bond

Stock Price	Equivalent Shares	Bond Value
$15	40	$ 600
20	40	800
25	40	1000
30	40	1200
35	40	1400

This can be expressed in graphic form, as in Figure 1.

Figure 1

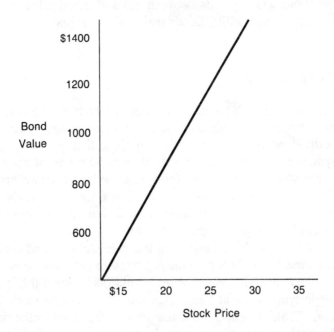

If the price of the bond were less than its value as shares of stock (share price times the number of shares into which it is convertible), then an opportunity to arbitrage would exist. The stock could be sold short, the bond purchased and converted into stock, and the stock used to cover the short position. The arbitrageur's profit would be the difference between the price of the convertible bond and the conversion value of the bond. Therefore, the potential for trading profits keeps the prices of the bond and stock aligned with one another.

A convertible bond may also trade at a price equal to its value as a "straight" bond. This is known as its investment value. In this case, you need to look at the relationship between the bond's coupon rate and the prevailing market interest rate for similar quality debt without the conversion feature. A 7% convertible bond maturing in 10 years will sell at least as high as the following prices, taking into consideration various market interest rate levels for straight debt issues of similar quality and maturity (see Table 4).

Table 4: Value of Convertible as Straight Debt

Market Interest Rate	Bond Coupon Rate	Bond Value
6%	7%	$1075
7	7	1000
8	7	935
9	7	870
10	7	815
11	7	760

As can be seen, when interest rate levels rise dramatically, the value of the convertible bond decreases. But it can only decrease to the point where the yield is comparable to a straight bond without the conversion feature. Even if the price of the common were to drop drastically, the value of the bond will stay at the bond market value floor, assuming the quality of the convertible doesn't deteriorate. This is shown in Figure 2.

Figure 2: Price Action of Convertible Bond

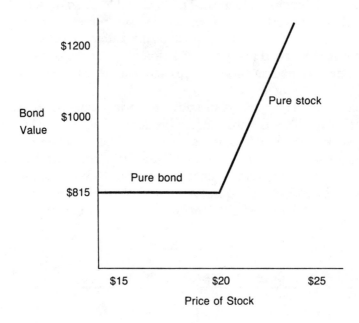

If interest rates go no higher than 10% and the common shares drop to $15, the price of the 7% convertible bond will fall. But it will hold at $815 and not drop to its stock conversion value of $600 ($15 times 40). At $875, the convertible bond begins trading as straight debt. This is the downside protection that's so important to total return investors.

Total return investors should note that because of their subordination to the issuer's more senior debt, convertibles have lower-quality ratings—usually a shade of a grade less—than their senior straight cousins. The Xerox sinking fund debenture 8.625% of 1999 is rated A+ by Standard & Poor's, while the company's convertible 6% of 1995 are only rated A. Similarly, the Ashland Oil sinking fund debenture 8.8% of 2000 is rated A and the convertible 4.75% of 1993 is rated A-. Lower ratings for the convertibles are a reflection of the fact that their owners stand further down the pecking order when it comes to the payment of interest and principal.

Convertible Bond Features

Convertibles have several important features. Most have mandatory sinking funds that retire two-thirds to three-quarters of the issue prior to maturity. As with so-called "straight" bonds, these redemptions ensure that the company will not be stuck with a balloon payment when the bonds mature. The sinkers start about one-third the way through the life of the bond and basically work the same way as they do with straight bonds. Either the company can buy bonds in the open market, or it can pay cash to the bond trustee who, in turn, randomly calls the requisite number of bonds to satisfy the sinking fund.

The issuing company can call the bonds for conversion after a certain period of time, usually two to three years from the date of issue, if specific conditions are met. Typically, the underlying stock must have traded for 20 (or 30) consecutive days at prices in excess of 140% (or 150%) of the conversion price. For example, a convertible bond with a conversion price of $20 (convertible into 50 shares) might be called if the underlying common trades at $30 or more for 20 days in a row. In this case, the bonds will be selling at $1,500 or more ($30 times 50 shares) with probably only a small conversion premium.

As explained earlier, if the price of the common stock moves up, the price of the convertible bond will rise also. At some point the conversion premium starts to close. That means the convertible price will not move up as fast as the common price. The premium approaches zero when the probability is very high that the issuing company will force conversion by calling the bonds. This price action is illustrated in Figure 3.

Pricing New Issue Convertibles

Why do companies issue convertible bonds in lieu of straight debt or common stock? In the first place, the bonds carry lower coupon rates than straight debt that's senior to it. Convertible debt is a cheaper means of raising capital. Secondly, if a company needs equity but doesn't want to dilute earnings by issuing more stock right away, it can sell "future" stock through the convertible medium. And it is sold at higher prices (therefore, at a cheaper cost to the company) because the conversion price is set above the common price. A final consideration for the issuing company is that interest payments on the bonds are tax deductible, whereas common stock dividend payments are not.

Figure 3: Size of Bond Conversion Premium as Price of Common Rises

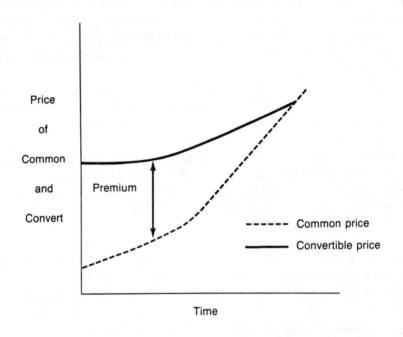

Although convertible bonds appear to offer the best of both worlds, the total return investor pays for these benefits. What the issuing corporation gains, the purchasing investor loses. When new issues are sold, the coupon rate of a convert will be lower than that of a comparable straight bond or debenture, and the conversion price will be set at a premium to the price of the underlying stock. Therefore, this hybrid security is more expensive to buy than either the company's common stock or straight bond, if each were purchased separately.

As a rule of thumb, most new convertible issues are sold with a conversion price set at a 15-25% premium over the share price, and a coupon rate of 2-4% less than a straight bond. The actual terms depend on the quality ratings of the new issue and demand for the bonds. When the issue size is small, institutional investors may ask for more concessions—a higher coupon or lower premium—because of poor liquidity in secondary markets. This sometimes makes these more speculative issues a better risk/reward value for individual investors, especially if the bonds are selling below par.

Table 5 shows typical differences in pricing terms for different quality issuers. Convertible bonds of a lower-quality company command considerably higher interest rates. But they also carry higher conversion premiums because the underlying stocks are perceived to have greater, albeit less certain, appreciation potential.

Table 5: Different Quality 20-Year Maturity Convertible Bond Issues

	High-Quality	Speculative
S&P/Moody's Rating	A/A	BB/Ba
Interest Rate	6%	9.5%
Issue Size	$100 million	$15 million
Conversion Premium	15%	20%

Secondary Markets for Convertible Bonds

Conservative total return investors shouldn't be led into a false sense of security by the investment value of a convertible bond, which is an estimate of how the bond would sell as a straight bond minus the conversion feature. The floor on the price of the bond can change over time as interest rate levels move up or down. Furthermore, the investment value depends on the issuer's creditworthiness—bonds of high-quality issuers provide a much more stable floor than those of low-graded issuers.

Here's an example of how the floor on the price of a convertible bond can change in a relatively short period of time while the level of interest rates stays the same. The specific bond was the Cooper Companies (formerly known as Coopervision, Inc.) 8.625's due 2005. This $195 million convert carries a B rating and is listed on the New York Stock Exchange.

The Cooper convert was trading in the $900 to $950 range at the beginning of 1987. With the stock at $16, the bond was clearly "out of the money" with a 55% conversion premium and 9% current yield. Cooper was experiencing problems with its contact lens business and was losing money. As the news got worse, the bonds slumped to the $750 level by mid-1987 even though the stock moved up to the high teens.

In this case, the convertible bond's perceived investment value deteriorated. It traded as a lower-rated straight bond with a current yield of 11.5% and an enormous conversion premium. Finally, Moody's Investor Service changed its ratings on Cooper's convertible bonds from a high B (B-1) to a low B (B-3), which is very close to a CCC rating. It cited Cooper's operating losses and uncertain outlook for future profitability as the reasons. Moody's was only confirming what the bond market had already known.

Prices of convertible bonds in the secondary market fluctuate more than those for straight bonds. As a total return investor, you may be the victim of a double-whammy effect if higher interest rates cause the stock and bond markets to fall together. The price of your convertible bond will not only drop in response to the action of the underlying common, but the floor will also drop due to higher interest rates. On the other hand, if interest rates fall, causing the stock market to rally, your convertible bonds will be blessed with the best of both worlds.

Evaluating Convertibles

Several rules of thumb should be followed when buying converts. First, don't put an order in to purchase one unless it sells for less than a 20% premium over conversion value. (Discount convertibles, which are an exception to this rule, will be discussed later.) In order to figure the conversion premium, use the following formula, where conversion value equals the market price of the underlying stock multiplied by the number of shares the bond is convertible into:

$$\text{Premium} = \frac{\text{Price of Bond} - \text{Conversion Value}}{\text{Conversion Value}}$$

For a bond convertble into 50 shares of common stock and selling at $1,150 when the stock trades at $20 a share, the premium works out to be the following:

$$\frac{\$1,150 - (\$20 \times 50)}{(\$20 \times 50)} = \frac{\$1,150 - \$1,000}{\$1,000} = \frac{\$150}{\$1,000} = 15\%$$

Therefore, if you bought the bonds for $1,150 and converted immediately into 50 shares, they'd be worth only $1,000. You'd forfeit the $150 premium paid. The higher the premium paid, the more you stand to lose in a forced conversion.

The second rule of thumb in buying converts is that you shouldn't pay too much above par value for a bond—certainly no more than $1,300. At higher levels the conversion premium begins to disappear. As this happens, gains in the stock price bring relatively less gain in the convertible price. Also, because the yield advantage over the common narrows when the convertible bond price is sky-high, you get much less downside price protection from the convert in weak markets.

Check to see when the issuing company can force conversion. If this happens right after you've paid a stiff premium for a bond, you'll end up an instant loser because the company only offers bondholders par value plus a small redemption premium. When your convertible trades way above par, there's a good chance the company will force you to convert if the bonds have no call protection. The issuer obtains a double benefit. It adds more equity to its balance sheet while at the same time eliminating the need to repay the debt.

An alternative way to evaluate convertibles is to calculate the number of years it takes to recover the conversion premium paid through the extra yield earned. This more sophisticated measure is known as the "time to breakeven." Many professional investors use this yardstick in analyzing the attractiveness of a convertible.

For example, if the issuer's common stock is yielding 3% and the convertible yields 9%, the difference is 6%. Given a conversion premium of 15%, it will take 2.5 years before the difference in yields is made up. As a rule of thumb, the shorter the time frame, the more reasonably priced the convertible. You should look for bonds where the conversion premium is recaptured through higher yields in three years or less.

Discount Convertible Bonds

Notwithstanding the previous discussion, total return investors will find situations where convertibles with large premiums are worth buying. These sell at discounts to par. They may offer greater rewards than convertibles selling at par or at slight premiums to par. A $100 price movement upward from a $850 bond (+11.8%) is greater percentage-wise than one from a $1,000 bond (+10%).

The convertible bonds of a company that's experiencing temporary financial difficulties are most likely trading at a steep discount to par, similar to the Cooper Companies converts mentioned earlier in the chapter. If they're subordinate to other long-term debt as well as short-term bank loans, they'll trade at an even deeper discount and higher current yield. Meanwhile, the conversion premium may have ballooned to 100%, 150% or even 200%, putting the bond "way out of the conversion money," to use a betting term. These are known as "busted" convertibles. They trade as straight bonds with conversion features that are no longer worth very much.

These discount converts merit investment attention because of the opportunity for price improvement to at least par value when the issuer's business fortunes turn around. And there's the possibility of appreciation beyond that point if the company emerges as a stronger entity. When the stock responds positively to the bullish news, hopefully the conversion feature will come alive again. While waiting, the total return convertible investor receives a high current return from interest payments and a "sky's the limit" in potential capital appreciation.

Discount convertibles actually trade at a slight premium to their investment value—the price at which the bond would sell for without the conversion privilege. The lower the premium, the better, as far as downside protection from further price drops is concerned. The investment value premium is figured by the following formula:

$$\frac{\text{Price - Investment Value}}{\text{Investment Value}} = \text{Investment Value Premium}$$

Assume the investment value of a 10% BB-rated straight bond is $825. A comparably rated discount convertible selling at $850 will have a low investment value premium of a shade under 3%.

$$\frac{\$850 - \$825}{\$850} = \frac{\$25}{\$850} = 2.9\%$$

Several studies conducted on the historical returns obtained from owner-ship of discount converts confirm that the deeper the discount from par value, the higher the return. This also held true for different quality con-vertibles, where lower-rated bonds outperformed better-rated bonds. In each study, total returns for discount convertible bonds outperformed the stock and bond market averages by more than 80% on an annual basis.

What made these generous returns possible? The market for discount convertible bonds is not very efficient. Institiutional investors ignore older convertible issues because they can't buy in size without disrupting the secondary market. Professional money managers would rather purchase new issue convertibles. They express their indication of interest to the un-derwriters by circling as many bonds as they want at par value.

Institutions have a tendency to liquidate holdings quickly when the prices of their convertible bonds drop much below par, particularly when the issuer is experiencing financial difficulties. With few individual inves-tors willing to take up the slack, the bonds languish at artificially low levels. Where are the contrarians?

As might be surmised, the perceived risks scare many investors away from discount convertible bonds. They're buying into troubled companies. But with adequate diversification among portfolio holdings, total return in-vestors should anticipate realizing their share of the above-average returns these bonds have historically produced.

Searching for Convertible Bonds

You might select one of three ways to go about prospecting for convert-ibles with attractive total returns. First, you may want to look for under-valued bonds—those with short paybacks characterized by relatively high coupons and low conversion premiums. After identifying several of these, analyze the prospects for each issuing company's common stock. Examine the financial statements, earnings trends, and its industry outlook. Follow the old adage of only buying the convertible if you like the common.

However, ferreting out convertibles with the best values is a time-con-suming job. The only alternative is to subscribe to a convertible bond statistical service or obtain copies of periodic studies that some of the larger stock brokerage firms put together on the intrinsic values of various convertibles. These provide basic data on the bonds including conversion premiums, current yields, yields to maturity, and breakeven times. You can screen them for likely candidates. This simplifies the task of selecting convertibles appropriate for total return investments.

The second approach is to buy convertible bonds of small growth companies. If earnings growth causes the underlying stock to increase in value, the bond price should follow suit. It's a lower-risk way to own a piece of these more speculative companies. And the rewards can be quite good once the company's financial achievements gain market recognition.

Because of the need to retain earnings to finance growth, no dividends will be paid on their common stocks. Smaller, unseasoned companies have to pay higher coupon rates on their convertible bonds than larger companies in order to compensate for the greater risks. Therefore, by purchasing the convertible bond, the total return investor will earn a good interest rate while waiting for the growth component to work its way into his bank account. Watch for these bonds when they're sold as new issues.

The third approach is a back-door strategy. Look for companies whose stock price has dropped due to temporary financial reverses or who have been out-of-favor with investors for some time. Then check to see if they have any outstanding convertible debt. If the common stock price is sufficiently depressed, the bond will usually sell at a sizable discount to par value. An earnings recovery should bring the convertible price back to par; if the common rallies in a major way, then the bond may move above par for even greater profits. In the meantime, you'll be getting a better current yield from owning the bond as opposed to the stock.

In order for this last strategy to work, you must do your homework. Investigate the prospects for recovery. Perform an interest coverage/cash flow analysis to ensure the company has the financial reserves to make the bond an eventual total return winner. Analyze what changes management has made to correct its operational problems. If your diligence pays off, you might come up with another Caterpillar convertible bond.

Caterpillar, Inc. is a heavy equipment manufacturing company with an agricultural bent. As a participant in these depressed industries in the mid-1980s, the company's profits sagged and investors neglected it. Caterpillar's BBB-rated convertible bond issue, the 5.5% of 2000, sold as low as $720 in 1984, where it held out a 7.6% current yield to those who were willing to bet on a turnaround.

Thanks to a massive cost cutting and plant and equipment upgrading, operating margins began to improve. Profits perked up in 1987 on only a small increase in sales. Caterpillar had tremendous leverage from its reduced overhead and more efficient manufacturing facilities. The stock took off. By September, 1987, the convertible bonds worked themselves all the way up to a price of $1,300. In three short years bondholders were rewarded with an average annual total return of approximately 32%. Not bad for an investment in a mundane company in a cyclical industry.

Whichever approach you decide on, never invest in a convertible security unless you like the prospects for the common stock, either as a growth or a turnaround company. Remember that in the final analysis, it's the positive outlook for the company, not the benefits of the convertible, that drives the price of the convertible security. As a total return investor, you want a good chance at capital appreciation in addition to the solid current returns that convertible investing delivers.

Convertible Preferred Stocks

Although the above discussion dealt with convertible bonds, a related type of investment, the convertible preferred stock, shouldn't go without mention as an excellent holding for total return investors. They represent about 25% of all the convertible securities outstanding. There's plenty of supply available and a variety of preferreds to chose from. One investor statistical service follows over 200 convertible preferred stocks.

Many convertible preferreds came into existence at the time of a corporate merger through which a tax-free exchange of convertible preferred shares for common stock was executed. The higher dividend yield on the preferred was an inducement for shareholders of the acquired company to complete the exchange. The 1986 merger of Sperry Corporation with Burroughs to create Unisys Corp. resulted in a mind-boggling, record-setting $1.4 billion issue of convertible preferred shares.

A convertible preferred stock has a designated par value per share (usually $10, $25, or $50), a fixed dividend, no maturity date, a conversion price, and a call price. Total returns are achieved much the same as with a convertible bond. In addition to obtaining a current yield higher than that available from the underlying common stock, the investor receives capital appreciation if the convertible preferred moves up in tandem with the stock.

Convertible preferred shares sell at yields averaging 1.5% less than straight preferred shares. As equity-type securities, convertible preferreds are not as secure as convertible bonds—interest on debt must be paid ahead of preferred dividends. The issuer is under no legal obligation to pay dividends, although with cumulative preferreds, any dividends in arrears must be paid ahead of common dividends. In addition, asset claims of preferred holders are subordinate to those of bondholders, but rank ahead of common shareholders.

All things being equal, the conversion premium on a convertible preferred will be less than that for a convertible bond. The lower premium reflects the market's perception that the preferred stock carries more risk than the bond. Convertible preferred shares are equity securities with characteristics more like common stock.

An important difference between convertible preferreds and bonds is the lack of a maturity date on the preferreds. This means that convertible preferreds carry greater interest rate risk than bonds. If interest rates rise and bond prices fall, the convertible bond will only drop so far before it eventually returns to par at maturity. With no maturity date, preferreds could remain depressed and never again trade at par value. However, some preferreds have a sinking fund schedule whereby a fixed number of shares are retired each year. This provides some price stability for those convertible preferred shareholders.

Figure 4 depicts what could happen if the preferred shares and bond each suddenly dropped 25% below their par value because the price of the common went into a tailspin. Without a recovery in the common price, the preferreds could sell at $18.75 forever, whereas the bond will eventually work its way back to par when it matures, assuming the company is financially healthy at that time.

Convertible preferreds do have some advantages. Dividends are paid four times a year, as opposed to semi-annual interest payments made on bonds. This feature offers a faster compounding of returns, particularly if they are held in a tax-deferred retirement account such as an IRA or Keogh plan. In addition, unlike bonds, you don't need a minimum of $1,000 to purchase convertible shares. They usually trade in a range of $10 to $50 a share and you can buy as few of them as you want.

In summary, the big money in convertible securities is made when the total return investor purchases bonds at a deep discount to par and waits until the issuer's financial prospects improve. Excellent total returns can

Figure 4: Price Comparison of Convertibles with and without Maturity Dates

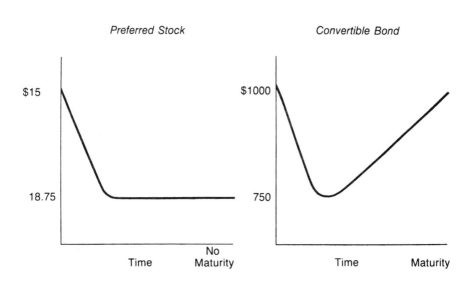

also be achieved with the purchase of convertible bonds selling for between $900 and $1,050, or for convertible preferreds trading around par.
These are securities of small or large capitalization companies with good
growth prospects. Fortunately, plenty of convertibles are available in these
price ranges to satisfy the total return investor's appetite.

Convertibles usually aren't purchased with the idea of holding them to
maturity. The investment goal is for the price of the underlying stock to
push the bond or preferred price up so the securities can be sold at a profit
in the secondary market. The quicker this happens, the greater will be the
annual total returns.

Once the conversion premium almost disappears, consideration should
be given to selling the bond. At price levels 30% to 40% above par, the
convertible price moves in tandem with the stock price. The bond loses

much of its total return appeal as its current yield diminishes. However, if you're still bullish on the stock, you may want to continue holding the high-priced convert because its yield provides more downside protection than that of the lower-yielding common. Whatever you do, be aware of the issuer's right to call the convertible securities to avoid being hit with a forced conversion.

Chapter 7

Total Return Limited Partnerships

Although limited partnerships used to be synonymous with tax shelters, many income-oriented ones make appropriate investments for total return investors who understand how they work. Limited partnerships are set up to hold and manage physical assets. They provide owners with good current returns and a chance for capital appreciation when partnership assets are sold. However, careful selection of limited partnerships is essential. Because they're not very liquid, you'll be married to them for quite some time.

Once known primarily for their tax shelter characteristics through the use of high leverage, the partnerships that are now in vogue are labeled as "economic" investments. They generate current returns as opposed to tax losses. The sponsors of income-oriented partnerships avoid using leverage to purchase assets; most cash flows go to the limited partners rather than to service debt.

Limited partnerships consist of a general partner (often referred to as the sponsor or syndicator) who controls the business and financial activities of the partnership, and limited partners who are passive investors. This latter group puts up most of the capital, but has limited liability with respect to the operation of the partnership.

The general partner is the most important ingredient to the success of this type of investment. It should be a financially-strong company with a solid net worth, experienced in the business activities of the partnership, and sport a good performance record. As with any venture, good management is the key to high total returns.

The limited partners' share of the partnership's profit and loss flows directly to them; there's no intervening layer of tax at the partnership level. Partnerships invest in a variety of business activities, including the acquisition and management of apartments, offices, shopping centers, mobile home parks, self-storage facilities, oil and gas wells, cable TV systems, nursing homes, hotels, and even fast food franchises.

Most income-oriented partnerships that would be logical total return investments are registered with the Securities and Exchange Commission as public offerings. These are sold through brokers and financial planners. The sponsors ususally set minimum investment amounts of $2,500 or $5,000, but lower these requirements to $2,000, or in some cases only $1,000, to accomodate the IRA and Keogh market. The partnerships also have investor suitability requirements of $20,000 to $30,000 in both net worth and gross income, or $60,000 in net worth alone, not including automobiles and home equity.

Limited partnerships provide several benefits to total return portfolios. They offer attractive current returns and the chance for some appreciation in the value of the underlying assets as a possible hedge against inflation. Partnership values are less volatile than stock prices and don't have to be monitored every day. These securities are meant to be held as long-term investments.

Even though the so-called economic partnerships don't provide tax losses, part of the distributions to limited partners is usually treated as a return of capital and isn't subject to tax. This sheltered portion could be as high as 25% to 35% of the amount paid out. Any tax savings are actually a tax deferral; you eventually pay taxes on the return of capital when the partnership is liquidated. Owners of pension plans and IRAs, of course, don't get any of their tax benefits because these retirement funds are already tax-deferred.

The major disadvantage of holding partnerships in your total return portfolio is lack of liquidity. Partnership owners must look on their investments as a long-term commitment. Some last for as many as 15 years before they're completely liquidated and the proceeds are paid to the limiteds.

Partnership interests are not actively traded like stocks on the New York Stock Exchange. You can't dump your investment in a hurry if you want to cash out at a reasonable price, or if it looks like the deal is going sour. Obviously, older persons should not load up their portfolios with limited partnerships unless they have a large amount of liquid assets they can get their hands on in a hurry.

Limited partnership interests may be sold before the partnership terminates, but the penalties are severe because of thin markets. You will need to contact your broker or financial planner for assistance. Some general partners have buy-back provisions where a small number of limited partner's interests are repurchased each year. This is most prevalent with the oil and gas income partnerships, but may also be found in some of the mortgage fund programs.

Several companies are in the market buying up "used" partnerships. These include Liquidity Fund of Emeryville, California and MacKensie Securities of San Francisco. A private outfit called the National Partnership Exchange (NAPEX) has also been established to facilitate trading in partnerships, but volume is low and it takes a while for a sell order to be matched with a purchaser. Trades are executed on the NAPEX through your broker on a commission basis.

Often the resale price of a limited partnership will be anywhere from 20% to 40% less than the liquidation value of the interest; the younger the partnership, the bigger the discount. Brokers and financial planners may solicit other clients to buy your partnership interest, but still expect to take a loss. The full benefits of partnership ownership are realized only when the securities are held to maturity.

The sponsors of some limited partnerships promise high payouts during their early years. Under tax reform, this passive income can be used to offset passive losses generated from old tax shelters. These higher-yielding partnerships appeal to persons with tax losses which can't otherwise be used. However, in many cases the underlying assets have low prospects for capital appreciation. Total return investors should avoid them.

Equipment leasing partnerships are a prime example. You get returns as high as 15% to 20% in the first few years (30% a year for those specializing in computer leasing). But when the partnerships are liquidated and assets sold, you only receive a fraction of your initial investment back. Depreciation and obsolescence have taken their toll. This capital erosion during the life of the partnership program reduces total return figures drastically.

In the past, sponsors of limited partnerships extracted a large percentage of your investment dollar in fees, commissions, offering expenses and such. In the case of leveraged partnerships, this totaled as much as 25% to 30% of the capital raised. With non-leveraged programs, fees and commissions amounted to 15% to 20%. In either case, this is a high price to pay, much higher than the 8.5% load charged on mutual funds sold through brokers.

High fees mean you have to wait a few years before the value of the investment increases enough to offset your up-front expenses. But fees are coming down to more reasonable levels due to competitive conditions in the syndication industry. And recently, several mutual fund organizations have introduced no-load (actually no sales charge) limited partnerships to the public though direct mail solicitation. They've been very successful raising funds this way.

Real Estate Partnerships

Certain types of real estate limited partnerships make appropriate total return investments. They can be purchased through brokers and financial planners or sometimes directly from the syndicator. Currently, the most popular are unleveraged real estate equity programs, mortgage loan partnerships with equity participations, and programs which combine the two, referred to as "hybrids." The investment characteristics of each are summarized in Table 1.

Table 1: Characteristics of Real Estate Partnerships

	Income	Growth	Risk
Unleveraged Equity Progams	Med-low	Med-high	Med
Participating Mortgages	High	Med-low	Med-high
Hybrids	Medium	Medium	Medium

No matter what type of real estate limited partnership you're considering, get a feel for the number and type of properties or mortgages to be bought, their geographic location (national or regional), and whether they are already existing properties or newly constructed ones. This data, when analyzed, will provide you or your advisor with additional information on the various risks associated with the investment.

Unleveraged public real estate partnerships take equity positions in a portfolio of apartment buildings, office buildings, shopping centers, business parks, warehouses, and even buildings housing fast-food restaurants.

A portfolio of properties is acquired in different geographical locations. Some syndicators specialize in a particular type of property, while others concentrate their purchases in one section of the country. The key point is that little or no debt is taken on to finance the properties in unleveraged real estate programs.

It's important to know what kind of acquisition prices the general partner is paying for properties. Real estate is priced on a capitalization rate which is sometimes referred to as the "cash on cash" yield. From a mathematical standpoint, it is the property's cash flow divided by purchase price. Cash flow is expressed as rents minus operating expenses, but excludes depreciation and financing costs. Table 2 shows a typical income statement for an unleveraged commercial property.

Table 2: Income Statement for Unleveraged Real Estate

Rents	$100,000
Less: Operating expenses	20,000
Cash flow	80,000
Less: Depreciation	20,000
Profit	$60,000

At a capitalization rate of 10%, this property would sell for ten times the $80,000 cash flow, or for $800,000. A lower cap rate would mean a higher price—at an 8% cap rate, the property would sell for 12.5 times cash flow or $1,000,000. Because of depreciation benefits, 25% of cash flow ($20,000 divided by $80,000) would be considered a tax-free return of capital. After front-end charges levied by the syndicator totaling 15% of capital raised, the net yield to a limited partner on a 10% cap rate property would be in the neighborhood of 8.5%.

Before investing in a real estate partnership, always ask what cap rates the general partner is paying for properties. Syndicators distribute beautiful pictures of what they're buying, but include very little data on property earnings, cash flows, and the fully-loaded price paid for them. If you can't obtain this important data or get straight answers to questions of acquisition costs, refuse to deal with the syndicator or the salesperson.

Unleveraged Partnerships

Unleveraged real estate partnerships offer total return investors modest current yields along with capital appreciation potential. An example of how a successful investment over a longer period of time might fare is shown in Table 3.

Table 3: Typical Unleveraged Real Estate Partnership Returns

Year	Current Income	Capital Appreciation	Total Return
1	5.5%	–	5.5%
2	7.0	1.0%	8.0
3	7.5	3.0	10.5
4	8.0	4.0	12.0
5	8.5	4.5	13.0
6	9.0	4.5	13.5
7	9.5	4.5	14.0

In this example, it's assumed that the real estate partnership was unspecified; no properties were bought by the general partner until all capital was raised. Further, it took one year to complete the purchases. During that time, investors earned money market rate of returns. Four apartment buildings were finally purchased at average capitalization rates of 8.25%. (A $1 million property delivered cash flows of $82,500 before interest expense, depreciation, and income taxes.)

In the second year, with all of the funds at work (less commissions and fees of 15%), investors earned a 7.0% current return (calculated as 8.25% times 85%) which was paid out as distributions. The properties appreciated a small amount during the year because they were upgraded with a series of capital improvements.

In the third year, through better operating controls and some rent increases, cash distributions to limited partners rose from 7% to 7.5%. Appreciation of the property values improved to a 3% annual rate, based on higher rents and cash flows. During years four through seven, the current income component increased at one-half percent a year on account of rent increases averaging 6% a year. Again, as rents increased, so did the value of the properties, although not as much because of increases in operating expenses due to inflationary factors.

The average annual total return generated from this hypothetical investment was close to 11%. This was the pre-tax return. Taxes on the part of the current income distributions not sheltered by depreciation (about 80% of the total) would be paid at the individual investor's tax rate, as would any capital appreciation. Therefore, after-tax returns would be several percentage points lower, or in the 9% range.

Of course, none of the capital appreciation was realized until the properties were sold. Most general partners of real estate syndications expect to hold onto properties for at least 7 to 10 years before selling them. At that time, the limited partners receive back their original capital and any appreciation, less funds set aside for the back-end participation of the general partner. This portion often equals 25% of any appreciation in the properties.

The actual investment results from an unleveraged real estate limited partnership depend on the management expertise of the general partner, the income producing potential of the properties purchased, the fees and expenses charged by the general partner, and the profit split between the general and limited partners. Results are also governed by the reasonableness of the price paid for the property, and the correctness of timing of the property sale.

Naturally you should review the past performance of the general partner, paying particular importance to cash flows and returns achieved on currently managed partnerships, the results of liquidating prior partnerships, and sales of individual real estate properties. These tables are found in prospectuses and offering materials, but are difficult to interpret; you may need the services of your investment advisor in this regard.

But you need to go beyond a review of past performance, particularly if the general partner specializes in a certain segment of the real estate market. You have to project industry supply and demand factors; if past returns were very high, competitors usually are attracted to the niche market. Recent investors in Public Storage limited partnerships found that out the hard way.

Public Storage builds and leases mini-warehouses to people for storing excess furniture, clothes, and odds and ends. A large demand for them comes from apartment renters, condo owners, and owners of newer homes where storage space is at a premium. The beauty of warehouses as an investment is that rent per square foot is the same as that for an apartment, yet construction costs are only one-half (you don't need to install plumbing, bathrooms, closets, kitchens, and so on).

Back in the early 1970s when mini-warehouses first came on the scene, Public Storage's limited partnership programs did very well. Their success spawned imitators and the competition heated up. By the mid-1980s, Public Storage had raised too much partnership money to invest profitably. The syndicator had to enter new geographic areas where it was not experienced building mini-warehouses. For the first time, it had to advertise for new tenants. Cash returns on Public Storage's later partnerships have been much lower than originally projected, leaving many investors extremely disappointed.

Using Moderate Leverage

Arguments are made over whether or not, in the face of low interest rates and relatively low property prices, leverage should be used in real estate syndications to enhance capital appreciation potential. Many recommend a modest amount of leverage, say between 25% and 35%. However, this concept is hard to sell as a result of negative press coverage of the soft real estate markets in various parts of the country. The average person would rather be more conservative and invest in totally unleveraged deals. Again, it's the contrarians willing to take a little more investment risk that stand to profit the most.

Table 4 shows the benefits of using moderate leverage with a property purchased at a 9% cap rate for $1,000,000. One syndicator uses all cash while the other leverages the property with 35% debt at a 10% interest rate.

The unleveraged purchase produces a 9% cash on cash current return, whereas the leveraged purchase earns a shade less than 8.5%. However, assuming the cash flow increases by $5,000 in year two and the capitalization rate stays the same, the value of the property increases by $45,000. For the unleveraged owner, this represents a 4.5% capital appreciation on the equity investment, but for the leveraged owner, it's almost a 7% jump. The leveraged owner gives up 0.5% current yield for a 2.5% advantage in appreciation. This demonstates how real estate total returns can be enhanced by financing part of the purchase price with debt.

Table 4: Leveraged versus Unleveraged Purchase of Real Estate

	Unleveraged	Leveraged
Purchase Price	$1,000,000	$1,000,000
Debt	0	350,000
Equity	$1,000,000	$ 650,000
Income Statement		
Rents	$125,000	$125,000
Expenses	35,000	35,000
Cash flow	90,000	90,000
Interest at 10%	0	35,000
Net cash flow	$ 90,000	$ 55,000

In a similar vein, some syndicators are being very creative by using zero-coupon financing to provide higher than normal current income during the early phases of a partnership. Zero-coupon mortgages are like zero-coupon bonds in that interest payments are deferred and added to the mortgage principal. This leveraging technique requires no current debt service and is attractive to total return investors seeking high yields. In addition, the IRS lets you recognize debt service accruals for tax purposes, which means a portion of the partnership's operating income is sheltered from taxes.

The problem with zero-coupon financing is that total return investors sacrifice capital appreciation for higher current income. When the partnership is liquidated, a large portion of the sales proceeds is used to pay down the mortgage. For example, in a completely leveraged deal, if the value of the assets doesn't appreciate in excess of the imputed interest rate on the zero-coupon mortgage, then there's nothing left for the equity owners at maturity. Even with 30% leverage at a 10% imputed interest rate, the property must appreciate at 4% a year. In addition, the rates for zero-coupon mortgages are higher than conventional rates in order to compensate the lender for taking higher risks.

Another popular limited partnership is the participating mortgage loan program. It offers relatively good current returns and the chance for a small amount of capital appreciation. With these mortgage partnerships, the limiteds not only receive current interest, but also a percentage participation of the increase in rental income or appreciation above a specified base. The property owner gives up some of the increase in the future value of the property in exchange for a lower interest rate on the loan.

Either participating first or second mortgage loans can be made. The second mortgage is riskier, but commands a higher rate of interest and greater participation in profits. In addition, the loan-to-value ratio is higher with a second mortgage, and it stands behind the first mortgage in the event of foreclosure.

As with unleveraged equity real estate partnerships, investors in the program should pay particular attention to promotional and management fees along with the profit split between the general partner and the limited partners. Because few syndicators have long track records in the participating mortgage loan business, it's diffcult to measure adequately past performance.

Hybrid Funds

The hybrid or balanced funds have been very popular with real estate syndicators since the Tax Reform Act of 1986 all but eliminated the sale of tax shelter deals. These funds combine all unleveraged equity real estate investments with mortgages. Some partnerships, like those offered by the Krupp group, also provide safety in the form of government-backed mortgage securities—guaranteed by Ginnie Mae or Fannie Mae—and future liquidity through the possible trading of partnership interests in the over-the-counter market.

For total return investors, the Krupp Cash Plus limited partnerships have been a big hit. Financial planners are selling them as a conservative investment with a capital appreciation kicker. Approximately 70% of the funds are invested in commercial real estate and the balance is invested in guaranteed mortgage-backed securities. The real estate is purchased on an all-cash basis with no debt.

Investors receive a relatively high yield from Ginnie Mae and Fanny Mae mortgage-backed securities whose underlying mortgages are guaranteed by agencies of the Federal government. A more modest current yield comes from the directly-owned real estate, but this has capital appreciation potential. And if rents go up, cash flows to the limited partners will also increase; this adds to the total returns.

Another fast-selling Krupp program is Krupp Insured Plus. It invests in participating mortgages whose interest and principal payments are guaranteed by the same agencies described above. These are new real estate financings developed by Ginnie Mae to encourage the partial or extensive renovation of mutlti-family housing. The partnership will share in rent increases above certain levels and the proceeds from the sale of the properties. It's hoped that the apartments will eventually be converted into condominiums and sold at a profit.

The total return comes by way of interest income from the mortgages and expected capital appreciation from property sales. In addition, the interest income should increase as rents rise and the participation feature kicks in. In contrast to many limited partnerships, the Krupp Insured Plus program provides for future liquidity; the interests are packaged as depositary receipts which will eventually trade in the over-the-counter market. Other syndicators are cloning these Krupp programs.

Vulture Funds

Several new types of real estate limited partnerships have come on the scene recently. One is the so-called "vulture" fund, which invests in financially-troubled properties with high vacancy rates, particularly those in the oil patch in the southwestern United States. The goal of these funds is to find physically good properties owned by distressed sellers in overbuilt markets. The syndicators then buy and hold them until the area's economy turns around and occupancy rates and rents increase to provide positive cash flows.

These funds have higher than normal front-end loads (in the 25% to 30% range), because the acquisition fees of the general partner are higher and more funds are set aside as reserves to support deficient cash flows from portfolio properties. Are these vulture funds risky? The risk is clearly higher than with all-cash purchases of fully leased buildings. These partnerships are for contrarians, where the prospects for substantial rewards are greater than from a bread and butter real estate investment. They are bought by patient investors who are willing to wait three to five years for the properties to turn the corner and become profitable.

Hotels

Another area that's caught the attention of real estate syndicators and investors alike are hotel partnerships. Hotel chain managements sell hotels to partnerships as a means of raising capital, similar to their franchising strategy of a few years ago. Hotels sell at cap rates that are 20% higher than other commercial property (approximately 11% versus 9%) because the ownership risks are greater.

Total return investors should realize that managing hotels is like running an operating business. This requires much more marketing and promotion savvy than managing an apartment building. Hotel room occupancy rates vary depending on a variety of factors, including competition, the business cycle, and travel patterns. However, with proper management, cash flows can be increased to make these limited partnerhips a worthwhile total return investment.

Nursing Homes

Nursing home ownership has also become a popular vehicle for limited partnerships, where high cap rates are also the norm. Here the risk is not low occupancy, but cutbacks in medicare payments, cost controls, or requirements imposed by governmental regulating authorities. The states issue certificates of need that limit the number of nursing homes in each area. With this artificially limited supply of beds and the greying of America, there's always very high occupancy rates in extended care facilities.

Nursing home operators try to obtain as many private pay residents as they can to lessen their reliance on medicare. Private pay patients are charged higher fees, which improves profit margins. However, investors should realize that as with hotels, nursing home partnerships are as much an operating business as the ownership of real estate. How profitable the business is will have a direct bearing on the price that will be realized when the property is eventually sold.

Oil and Gas Income Partnerships

The general partners of these income-oriented partnerships purchase existing oil and gas reserves, manage property operations, sell the hydrocarbon production, and then distribute the proceeds to limited partners. They usually don't drill new wells on their properties, but sometimes workover existing ones when production declines. Better-managed oil and gas deals should net investors 12% to 15% annual discounted cash flows during the life of the partnership.

Actual returns from these income partnerships depend on well production, the price of oil and gas, the accuracy of the recoverable reserve count, and the amount of partnership reserves depleted each year. The depletion is real, for oil and gas assets are a wasting resource. Part of the cash flows to limited partners is considered a return of capital, sheltered from taxes through the depletion allowance. But you won't have any investment principal left at the end of the partnership when all oil and gas reserves have been recovered and sold.

What this boils down to is that total return investors should only invest in these partnerships if they believe the price of oil will go up. If it does, this not only increases cash flow but allows the general partner to rework existing wells and drill new wells to capture more reserves. Together, the net effect of higher prices is to provide investors with higher than expected current returns, or a chance for capital appreciation if they sell out their partnership interest early.

A typical oil and gas income program produces high cash flows in the first few years, which decline as production from each well drops off. Revenues may increase, of course, if the price of oil and gas escalates the way it did during the early 1970s. The graph of the cash flows of a 10-year oil and gas income partnership, assuming an oil price hike in the fifth year, looks like Figure 1.

Ever since the early 1980s, the price of energy resources has been quite volatile. After rising to $38 a barrel, oil dropped to $10 then recovered to $20. And the outlook is uncertain. Expectations of future prices, however, are factored into how much syndicators are willing to pay for oil and gas reserves at the time the income partnerships are formed.

Although oil and gas have provided a good hedge against inflation in the past, their prices haven't kept pace recently, and there's no assurance they will in the future. World energy reserves are dropping, which may allow the oil and gas business to stage a comeback a few years hence. According to one syndicator, oil and gas prices and supplies run in 15-year cycles and the industry is now at the bottom. After prices eventually rise, investment funds become plentiful and a pick-up in drilling occurs. This, in turn, leads to an oversupply of oil and gas and falling prices.

Figure 1: Returns from an Oil and Gas Income Program

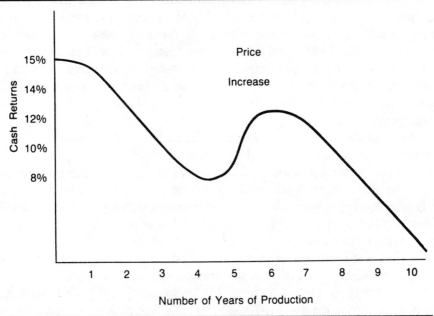

The general partner's expertise in evaluating, selecting, and pricing acquisitions will be a key factor in the success of any oil and gas investment. Properties are bought on a discounted cash flow basis to establish a fair market price for reserves. During periods of weak oil and gas prices, some general partners will locate distress sales of hydrocarbon reserves. If the properties are efficiently managed, they'll generate good yields for the limiteds.

Investor returns from income funds also depend on the front-end costs of buying into the partnership (sales and property acquisition fees), management fees during the life of the partnership, and the revenue/expense sharing arrangement between the general and limited partners. The general partner may take 10% to 15% of partnership income in addition to its 15% management fee.

It should be pointed out that some oil and gas income funds ran into financial difficulties by borrowing to purchase reserves just as the oil boom peaked in the early 1980s. As the price of oil dropped and the reserve estimates proved to be over-optimistic, these partnerships experienced a severe cash flow crunch. The problems of Petro-Lewis are well-known to many investors.

As with other limited partnerships, oil and gas programs are not liquid. They must be held for a long time, often up to 15 years or more until the wells run dry. However, some general partners offer their limited partners annual presentment rights, whereby they repurchase a small number of partnership interests each year at a slight discount to reserve value. Notwithstanding the illiquidity aspects, oil and gas does provide another avenue of diversification for total return investors and can serve as an inflation hedge if oil and gas prices resume their upward climb, causing other prices to follow suit.

Cable TV Partnerships

A final category of limited partnerships appropriate for total return investors are cable TV partnerships. They've become popular of late because of the industry's tremendous growth potential. Cable provides total return investors current income and an opportunity for capital appreciation, along with added diversification for the portfolio.

Cable TV lends itself to the partnership form of business because of its high cash flows. Systems in the more rural areas of the country, where TV is the major source of entertainment, have done quite well over the years. Construction costs are lower than in the big cities and because cable TV is the "only game in town," subscriber turnover rate is low. Lastly, recent cable deregulation gives system owners greater latitude in raising rates without regulatory approval.

The general partner buys cable systems and hopes to increase cash flows through better management of the systems. This includes increasing the number of subscribers with more intensive marketing, adding channels and premium services such as Home Box Office and Disney, building the system to outlying areas not served, and raising rates. The higher the cash flow, the greater the price received when the system is eventually sold.

Cable TV partnerships most suitable for total return investors are either unleveraged or use moderate leverage. The former provides more immediate cash flow benefits while the latter offers higher capital gain potential. In either case, due to high system depreciation benefits, most of the cash flows will be sheltered in the early years of the partnership. Because depreciation deductions are eventually recaptured as income when the systems are sold (similar to equipment leasing), total returns from cable programs are tax insensitive—they're about the same for both individual and tax-deferred pension investors.

A typical unleveraged cable TV partnership will produce the returns shown in Table 5.

Table 5: Total Return for Cable TV Partnerships

Year	Current Income	Capital Appreciation	Total Return
1	5.5%	–	5.5%
2	8.0	3.0%	11.0
3	9.0	3.0	12.0
4	10.0	3.0	13.0
5	11.0	3.5	14.5
6	11.5	3.5	15.0

Higher increases in returns are generated in the first few years as the sponsor upgrades the system, adds subscribers, and improves revenue and profit margins. As with real estate partnerships, the capital appreciation component isn't realized until the cable system is sold.

Both current income and capital gains depend on prices paid for cable TV systems. The higher the price, the less the returns unless good revenue and cash flow improvement can be generated by the new management. The prices for cable TV systems have gone way up in the wake of cable deregulation and increased investor interest in owning these properties.

In summary, total return investors should pick only those limited partnerships that offer attractive current yields paid for completely out of cash flows, plus the opportunity for capital appreciation. The amount of gain will depend on the leverage used. Limited partnerships are long-term investments with very little liquidity.

The next chapter discusses other securities that are suitable for the total return investor. One is called the master limited partnership, which is a more liquid partnership that's become very popular of late with the investing public.

Chapter 8

Other Total Return Securities

Several other types of securities are worth considering as total return investments. They're not as well-known to the investing public as the stocks, straight bonds, convertible securities, and limited partnerships discussed in prior chapters. These securities might be characterized as more conservative holdings with good risk-reward ratios. They include real estate investment trusts, master limited partnerships, written call options, and the Americus Trust shares. Each one offers relatively high current income with opportunitites for capital appreciation.

Real Estate Investment Trusts

An almost ideal security for total return investors is the real estate investment trust (REIT). Well-managed ones have produced excellent results over the years. REITs are similar in many respects to real estate limited partnerships in that the trust advisors buy and manage properties or make mortgage loans and distribute the cash flow to shareholders. When most of the income is paid out, no income taxes are due at the trust level.

A long battle has been waged to overcome the negative image of REITs. In the mid-1970s, the value of REIT assets plunged by 60% and many investors suffered huge losses in share values. The main problem was with unseasoned mortgage REITs making a lot of bad loans to construction companies. Now the tide has turned and REITs are staging a comeback. Even smaller institutional investors who don't have the resources to buy investment-grade real estate directly are starting to nibble at REIT shares.

At mid-1987, over 175 REITs of all varieties were active participants in the real estate market. At least 40 of them have market capitalizations in excess of $100 million, which represents good liquidity for all investors.

One of them, Rockefeller Center Properties, has a market value of over $800 million and its shares trade on the New York Stock Exchange.

The big advantage REITs have over real estate partnerships is liquidity—you can buy and sell their shares (technically called shares of beneficial interest) just like any other publicly-traded stock. This feature makes them particularly suitable for total return investors who want portfolio exposure to the real estate sector, but are reluctant to sacrifice liquidity. This doesn't mean you trade REITs for quick profits. Total return investors should plan on holding REITs for at least a three to five-year period to protect against having to sell in a weak stock or real estate market.

Tax reform had no impact on real estate investment trusts. They never were considered as vehicles to shelter income from taxes. REIT advisors always had to use lengthly depreciation schedules on their properties and never used much leverage. Tax reform has established a level playing field where REITs are just as attractive a vehicle as limited partnerships for the ownership of real estate.

Because REITs distribute almost all their cash flows as dividends and pay no income tax on earnings, their current yields are much higher than average yields for other stocks. This compensates for their somewhat lower price appreciation potential compared to the stocks of companies that retain a large portion of earnings for future growth.

Not surprisingly, REITs have done as well or better than the stock market with respect to total returns. They've averaged 18.2% compared to the S&P 500's 17.8% over the last seven years. More importantly, their returns have been much more consistent than the S&P 500, indicating less volatility. This is illustrated in Table 1.

As can be observed from the chart, REITs have not performed as well in the last two years as the S&P 500. Many investors carried negative feelings toward the real estate industry because of overbuilding, high vacancy rates, and and financial difficulties experienced by some companies. Compared to the stock market, real estate clearly lost its investment appeal in 1985, 1986 and the first half of 1987

However, during the 1987 stock market crash, REITs fared much better than most other industry groups. In that fateful third week of October, 1987, REIT stocks were off just 11.0% compared to the drop in the S&P 500 of 22.9%. This amply illustrates their defensive characteristics in down markets.

Table 1: Comparison of REIT Annual Total Returns with Other Stocks

Year	Equity REITs	S&P 500
1980	17.2%	31.5%
1981	7.5	(4.9)
1982	17.0	20.4
1983	31.3	22.3
1984	17.2	6.0
1985	18.4	31.0
1986	18.5	18.6
Average	18.2%	17.8%

Source: National Association of Real Estate Investment Trusts (NAREIT).

In the best of worlds, REIT dividends will increase at a steady pace as the trust's advisors raise rents on existing real estate holdings, or as more properties are acquired. REIT managements tend to hold properties for the long term; they will sell them only when better opportunities present themselves for increased trust earnings. It's the high current yield, plus future share price and dividend increases that make these worthwhile total return investments.

REITs also provide a hedge against inflation as long as the supply and demand for the rental property a REIT owns remain in balance. As with real estate limited partnerships, most REITs specialize in certain types of properties or a geographical area. Before committing funds, potential investors must look closely at the property portfolio of each REIT to get a flavor for its composition.

Finite Real Estate Investment Trust

The finite real estate investment trust (FREIT) has become popular in recent years. Unlike the more common perpetual trust, which theoretically goes on forever, the managers of a finite trust plan to sell off properties and liquidate the FREIT in 5 to 10 years. FREITs were designed to overcome the stock market's reluctance to fully value the properties in a REIT portfolio. REITs often sell at a discount to the actual market value of their real estate holdings. With a FREIT, these values hopefully will be realized fully by shareholders when the properties are liquidated and cash proceeds distributed to them.

Most FREITs are new on the investment scene. They have little or no performance history. Furthermore, it's not clear how many years it will take to liquidate portfolios since real estate is a cyclical industry. Some FREITs may continue for only 4 or 5 years, while others may go on for 10 to 15 years.

Equity REITs

Equity REITs, as the name implies, take ownership positions in real property as opposed to being strictly mortgage lenders. Therefore, management is an important consideration in selecting them as investments. The best ones to invest in are those that create value for their shareholders. This is done primarily by upgrading and refurbishing properties, finding better uses for a property, or reducing property expenses. The name of the game is to boost cash flows and property values.

Several equity REITs have been sucessful in this endeavor. United Dominion Realty of Richmond, Virginia, has done this with apartment houses in the Virginia/North Carolina area. Federal Realty is another example of a REIT with a value-added philosophy. It specializes in renovating older strip and community shopping centers in the mid-Atlantic and southeastern parts of the United States.

A company with a particularly noteworthy record is Weingarten Realty, a shopping center operator in Texas. Despite the overbuilt Texas real estate market and weak economy, Weingarten management has maintained occupancy rates, increased revenues, and boosted trust earnings per share—quite an achievement when other real estate owners are going bankrupt in the oil patch.

REIT earnings can grow through reinvestment of retained earnings not paid out (usually only a small amount) or from higher cash flows from existing properties. The trust advisor may also sell new shares to raise additional equity capital. The proceeds are then used to purchase more properties either with or without leverage. The ability of the REIT to buy attractively priced real estate with low-cost blended capital adds to its growth rate.

Financial leverage reduces cash flow available for dividends because of the necessity of servicing the debt. But if the properties are well-managed, then the dividend and share price should rise at a faster percentage pace than for non-leveraged REITs. Table 2 demonstrates the difference in total returns between leveraged and unleveraged REITs.

Table 2: REIT Total Returns

	Current Yield	Dividend/ Share Price Growth	Total Return
Leveraged	5.5%	7.0%	12.5%
Unleveraged	8.0	3.0	11.0

The total return for leveraged real estate is made up of a smaller current dividend but a larger capital gain component. Its projected total return is also higher than that for the unleveraged one. This compensates investors for the inherent greater risk of the leveraged REIT due to its debt load. These fixed costs must be covered whether vacancies are up or down.

Mortgage REITs

Pure mortgage REITs cannot be considered as total return investments, because under normal conditions they provide only one component, current yield. Capital appreciation is only be realized if the REIT holds a portfolio of long-term, high-yield mortgages, and interest rates move downward causing the trust's shares to be bid up in price. This did happen in 1982, when the NAREIT index of mortgage REITs produced a total return of 42.3%. But don't expect a repeat performance of that magnitude any time soon.

However, one type of mortgage REIT specializes in participating mortgages and qualifies as a total return investment. This REIT receives a fixed return from the mortgage, plus a portion of any rent increases above a certain point. Therefore, if the mortgaged properties perform well, cash flow and dividends will increase, and the REIT share price should move up on the strength of higher payouts.

Health care REITs owning a portfolio of participating mortgages are excellent total return investments. Recently, a number of nursing home and hospital management companies have spun off their health care properties into REITs. The facilities are subsequently leased back to the operating company on a fixed rent formula plus a percentage of any revenue growth over a base amount. Although the REITs own the properties, this arrangement is similar to the income stream of a participating mortgage.

The rentals are supported by government health care reimbursements and leases are structured on a triple net basis, where the renter pays all costs such as property taxes, insurance, electricity, and heat. The typical health care REIT may participate in 5% of the year-to-year increases in gross revenues from the facility. And if it can successfully introduce some leverage into the sale-leaseback transactions, then dividends will rise at an even faster pace.

Master Limited Partnerships

One investment medium that has gained popularity with both issuers and investors alike are master limited partnership (MLPs). They're publicly traded partnerships whose owners enjoy both flow-through income benefits and liquidity. Master limited partnerships are similar to limited partnerships sold by syndicators, but they have the one distinct advantage of being actively traded in the secondary markets.

The Tax Reform Act of 1986 has provided an additional incentive for corporate management to consider the partnership form of organization. Before tax reform, individual rates were higher than corporate rates; afterwards, the reverse became true. That's because although corporate rates were reduced, they didn't drop as much as individual rates. Shareholders now benefit when a corporation is converted to partnerships. With a top individual rate of 33% (28% for most people) and 34% for corporations, it makes more sense to have individuals rather than corporations pay taxes on company earnings.

MLPs are usually the result of either "roll-ups," where many illiquid partnerships are combined and exchanged for publicly traded units, or "roll-outs," where a company spins off assets to shareholders. In either case, the parent company or sponsor usually takes over as general partner and manages the master limited partnership on behalf of the limited partners. Sometimes a whole corporation is transformed into a master limited partnership without any rolling. From a technical standpoint, MLP interests are represented by depositary receipts that are freely traded on the stock exchanges or in the over-the-counter market.

The first master limited partnership was created by Apache Petroleum in 1981, when it rolled up more than 30 limited partnerships into a single MLP. Apache was followed by other MLPs in the oil and gas industry and several in the real estate industry, the first being Southwest Realty Partners.

Curiously, both Apache and Southwest have fallen on hard times. Apache's shareholder distributions have been cut severely because of low oil and natural gas prices and too much partnership debt. In the case of Southwest Realty, which has all of its holdings in economically depressed Texas, no current distributions are being paid and several of its apartment properties are in bankruptcy.

Recently, a great variety of master limited partnerships have come to market. These include Burger King Investors (fast food restaurants), Freeport McMoRan Partners (sulphur and phosphate recovery), Jones Intercable Investors (cable TV), and even the world-famous professional basketball team, the Boston Celtics Limited Partnership. In fact between 1982 and June, 1986, $2.6 billion has been raised through the MLP format in the public markets; another $4 billion was sold between July, 1986 and June, 1987.

All MLPs provide relatively high current returns because earnings are not taxed at the partnership level. In addition, part of the dividend is usually sheltered by depreciation or depletion allowances, and is considered a return of capital not subject to current income tax. However, the tax is really deferred because the return of capital portion of all dividends received during partnership ownership should be subtracted from the shareholders' basis (purchase price) when the shares are sold. Capital gain is calculated on the reduced cost.

If all MLP cash flow from an operating business (as opposed to asset management) is paid out to limited partners, then none is left to plow back into the business. Any earnings retained will be taxed to the partnership level. This limits growth in earnings as well as the capital appreciation component of the total return equation. Most master limited partnerships must rely on greater usage of their assets at higher prices in order to increase cash flows.

As with other limited partnerships, total returns from MLPs consist of high current dividends plus expected capital appreciation from growth in distributions or through higher valuations of the business. However, some master limited partnerships hold depleting assets; distributions will eventually have to be reduced unless the general partner can add reserves to the asset base or asset valuations increase. The oil and gas industry is a prime example of this phenomenon.

A successful master limited partnership's total return might look like Table 3 which assumes that the market price multiple of each dollar of partnership earnings stays the same, and that asset value growth equals share price growth. Notice that the yields are high but increase slowly. This is typical of most unleveraged MLPs.

Table 3: MLP Total Returns

Year	Current Yield	Asset Value Growth	Total Return
1	10.00%	2.5%	12.50%
2	10.25	2.5	12.75
3	10.50	2.5	13.00
4	10.75	2.5	13.25
5	11.00	2.5	13.50

One problem that you should be aware of is that many new MLPs start out by distributing funds in excess of cash flow from operations. This results in an artificially high current yield. It's an inducement to get investors to buy a new issue or to exchange assets. Either the excess is guaranteed by the general partner or it's paid from partnerhsip reserves. In any event, high payouts usually only last a few years. After that, the MLP distributions must stand on their own and be supported by whatever the cash flow turns out to be.

For instance, consider Freeport-McMoRan Resource Partners, a master limited partnership listed on the New York Stock Exchange. It's a roll-out of Freeport-McMoRan's phosphate, sulphur, geothermal and uranium businesses, wherein the parent retained about 80% ownership of the partnership. The public owns 20% and is guaranteed an annual $2.60 distribution per unit for five years. However, the partnership started out by producing cash flow of only $1.80 or 70% of the distribution. The balance was paid out of cash flow attributable to the parent's shares.

Unless the Freeport partnership can increase earnings to cover the distribution, it will have to be cut and the limited partners will undoubtedly suffer when the unit price drops. Those investors owning Freeport units are betting on a future upturn in the agricultural economy, the main source of Freeport's customer base.

Another concern with MLPs is how the IRS and eventually tax writers in Congress come down on the proliferation of master limited partnerships. The IRS in the past has argued that because these securities are freely traded, they're not partnerships in the true sense of the word (businesses must meet two of four conditions in order to qualify as a partnership for pass-through treatment). They believe MLPs are really stocks. It's the old argument that if it walks like a duck and quacks like a duck, it probably is a duck.

What's behind the IRS position is that the Federal government is losing money by not being able to tax the revenues from these partnerships twice, the way they do with corporate earnings and dividends paid to stockholders. The IRS feels the proliferation of master limited partnerships is eroding the corporate tax base.

Congress has rejected the IRS arguments several times in the past. But with the growth of new partnerships and particularly the conversion of many companies from a corporate form of organization to the master limited partnership structure, IRS arguments may carry greater weight, particularly when the Federal government is looking for more ways to raise revenue. This debate is a red flag for MLP total return investors.

At a minimum, the IRS hopes to have all income from master limited partnerships declared as portfolio income as opposed to passive income. This means that investors with tax shelter losses will not be able to use the taxable portion of their income from the MLPs to offset passive losses. But Congress may limit the MLP format to those businesses that have traditionally been organized as partnerships such as real estate and the extractive industries (oil and gas). Other existing MLPs may be grandfathered. This would be the most positive outcome for many master limited partnerships already in existence.

In the final analysis, it appears potential tax law changes will always cloud MLP status to a certain extent. This uncertainty is another reason why the current yields on these securities are so high, providing the opportunity for attractive total returns to investors who chose the right MLPs.

Writing Call Options

Another technique you can use to increase total return income is to write covered call options on common stocks you own. This limits both risk and return, but is popular with more conservative investors. Total returns are achieved through a combination of dividend income, option writing income, and capital appreciation, although the latter is usually limited to small gains.

A call is the right to purchase 100 shares of stock at a certain price for a fixed period of time. The call becomes worthless if it expires unexercised. Holders of shares who sell calls on them receive a premium (the price of the call) in exchange for granting this privilege. The call option writer is still entitled to dividends on the underlying stock.

If you own a stock for which calls trade on one of the option exchanges, you can sell either a three-, six-, or nine-month call on it. You take in the call premium and still collect any dividends that are paid on the stock while you still own it. The call premium can amount to 3% to 4% of the stock price, a nice bonus in addition to dividend income.

The call or striking price may be below, at, or above the current price of the stock. Because you really don't want the call exercised and the stock bought out from your total return portfolio, it's usually best to sell a call with a strike price a bit above the price of the common. If the call expires, you write another on your shares and start the process all over again.

Your greatest risk is that the stock advances in price and is called away from you. In this case, you won't profit from any price appreciation above the call price. But you do get to keep as profit the difference between what you paid for the stock and the call price.

Another risk, of course, is that the price of the stock will decline. Fortunately, the call premium you receive offsets part of that decline. In any event, you're usually not too concerned with short-term downward price movements of stocks in your total return portfolio. Remember, you're supposed to be holding securities for the longer-term.

Here's how the call writing technique works. (No provision for commissions or other transaction costs is taken into account.) Assume you own 100 shares of a stock which sells for $28 a share. You sell a 6-month call for $2 a share or $200 at a strike price of $30 a share. The stock pays a $1.50 dividend for a 5.4% yield. If the price stays the same and the call expires unexercised, then you have a total return of $200 from the call and $75 from half a year of dividends. Doubling this $275 6-month return to $550, your annualized total return on the $2,800 investment becomes 19.7%, as shown in Table 4.

Table 4

	Dividend Yield	Premium Income	Capital Appreciation	Total Return
Six-month income	$75	$200	–	$275
Annual per cent	5.4%	14.3%	0.0%	19.7%

If the stock goes up to $35 and the call is exercised, then your 6-month return is $475 (add in the $200 profit), or 34.0% on an annualized basis. This is shown in Table 5.

Table 5

	Dividend Yield	Premium Income	Capital Appreciation	Total Return
Six-month income	$75	$200	$200	$475
Annual per cent	5.4%	14.3%	14.3%	34.0%

Of course when that happens, you lose the opportunity for an additional $500 profit. Had you not written the call and sold the stock at $35, your total return would have been 55.4% on an annualized basis.

On the other hand, if the price of the stock drops from $28 to $25, then your $3 loss has been cushioned by the $2 proceeds from the call, which will expire unexercised under this scenario. Your annualized total return, assuming you sold the stock after six months, is shown in Table 6.

Table 6

	Current Yield	Premium Income	Capital Depreciation	Total Return
Six-month income	$75	$200	$(200)	$(25)
Annual per cent	5.4%	14.3%	-21.4%	-1.7%

Call premiums vary with the volatility of the underlying common stock. The greater the historical price fluctuations of the shares, the larger the premium as a percentage of the stock price. With higher volatility, there's greater chance for profit for a call buyer so he's willing to pay more for this privelege. Conversely, lower call premiums are associated with less volatile stocks.

More aggressive total return investors who want to purchase growth shares which pay low or no dividends can reduce their risks by writing call options on them. Most total return investors, however, will be satisfied with earning a few extra percentage points by writing calls on more stable, higher-yielding stocks. They don't want the aggravation of worrying about shares being called away from them.

There's one final point to bear in mind when dealing in options. You'll pay high commission costs when selling both a single call (up to 10% of its price) and the underlying stock, if the call is ever exercised (up to 3%). Because this could eat up a lot of the profit when writing one call, it's usually best to write several at once. You'll need ownership of a few hundred shares of a particular stock, which means your portfolio holdings must be relatively large before you employ this technique. In order to keep transaction costs down, you could also use the services of a discount broker, or negotiate lower commissions with your full-service broker.

Americus Trust Shares

Other lesser-known variations of equity securities may also be particularly suitable for total return investors. The Americus Trust stocks are a case in point. The Americus Shareowner Service Corporation in New York City takes the stock of a large capitalization company and splits it into separate income and capital gains components through the formation of a unit trust. Investors may buy either unit depending on their investment objectives.

Getting this concept approved by the regulatory agencies was not easy for the Americus firm. It took seven years to obtain the blessings of the Internal Revenue Service and Securities and Exchange Commission. The New York Stock Exchange refused to list Americus securities, other than that of the bellwether AT&T issue, because of corportate opposition to creating two classes of shareholders with competing interests. However, the American Stock Exchange finally bought off on the idea.

Here's how the Americus unit trust works. One set of trust holders, known as the Prime owners, receives all dividends from the underlying shares plus a small portion of capital gains. The other group, called the Score owners, receives appreciation of the underlying shares above a certain level, but no dividend income. Score shares are similar to a five-year warrant or option.

The income components are ideal holdings for the more conservative total return investors. These persons receive dividends which are higher than those of the underlying stocks, yet also have a chance at a limited amount of capital gain. And all the unit trusts are made up of shares of large blue chip companies that are relatively stable.

An example of how total return investors benefit from this arrangement can be illustrated by reciting the history behind the first Americus Trust—the one set up for AT&T in 1983. The trust holds shares of all seven regional Bell companies plus the new AT&T company. Shareholders of the old AT&T who chose to exchange their pre-breakup shares for Americus units could then divide them into Prime or Score shares.

At the time of the breakup, the Prime shares were selling for $58-$60 and the Score shares were selling for $8 a piece. The Prime yielded 9.3%

compared to a yield of 8.3% on the AT&T units. Prime holders received all the income on AT&T and sister company shares for five years and any share price gains up to $75 a share. Score unitholders received all appreciation beyond $75 a share.

By 1987, the Americus AT&T units were trading at $110 to yield 5.7%, while the Prime component was selling at $78 and yielding 8%. Meanwhile, the Score component units shot up from $5 to $32 a share. Notice that the sum of the value of the two components just about equals the unit price; it stays that way as long as arbitrageurs can profit from any price discrepancies. The approximate total returns for the Prime shareholders are shown in Table 7.

Table 7

	Current Return	Capital Appreciation	Total Return
1984	7.0%	–	7.0%
1985	7.5	10.0%	17.5
1986	8.0	20.0	28.0

The average total return works out to about 17.5% a year—not too bad for as conservative an investment as AT&T and the regional telephone companies. Of course, future returns are limited by the $75 cap on the value of the shares when the trust is dissolved in 1988. It should be pointed out that the Score shares did extraordinarily well, scoring a 540% gain in the three years of their existence.

Because of the success of the AT&T issue (there are six million units outstanding), the Americus people have come out with 27 more issues, all tied to the stocks of blue chips companies. However, the current yields are not as high compared with the AT&T issue because the yields on the underlying shares are lower.

Here's how the Sears deal is set up. Holders of Sears, Roebuck and Co. common shares can exchange them for units of Americus Trust for Sears Shares. They may keep either component, sell the other one, and reinvest the proceeds in the component they wish to hold. Other investors may purchase Prime or Score components in the secondary market. The termination claim of $64 a share lasts until July, 1992.

Prime holders get all appreciation up to $64, while Score holders are entitled to any price appreciation of the common stock beyond that point. While the Sears common pays a $2.00 dividend, the Prime holders receive $1.95 (a 4.5 cent annual sponsor and trustee fee is subtracted). However, when the Sears stock is selling at $53 and yielding 3.8%, the Prime units sell for $37 to yield 5.3%. That's a 1.5% premium in current return over the underlying shares. Given this pricing scenario, the Score units will trade in the $17 range.

The question arises, why invest in Americus Prime shares rather than directly in the blue chip stocks? The answer is that the former securities offer a more conservative investment—Prime shares are less volatile than the common shares. Also, ownership of the Prime shares means maximizing benefits from any dividend increase, as all of it flows to the Prime shareholders. Some sophisticated investors see the Prime shares with their potentially higher yield to maturity as a good substitute for a preferred stock or a five-year bond investment.

Over a period of time, total returns may be the same for the common shares and the Prime, but the lower risk of the Prime shares make them more desirable for total return investors. The only negative is the opportunity cost of not having an unlimited participation in the rise of the common stock, and then seeing its price take off due to a combination of an earnings speed-up and a higher price-earnings ratio.

This ends the discussion and analysis of the different types of securities that are appropriate holdings for total return investors. The next chapter will review the various options for implementing the total return strategy to put you on the path to investment success.

Chapter 9

Implementing a Total Return Strategy

Now that you've learned all you need to know about total return investing, along with the type of securities that are right for your portfolio, you'll want to implement the strategy. Before starting, you'll need to establish investment goals and objectives suitable to your own particular circumstances.

You can be an aggressive or conservative total return investor, or follow a course that's somewhere in between. The amount of risk you're willing to assume will vary depending on your tolerance for it, your investment experience, and the type and amount of investment assets under consideration.

Probably the most important factor to consider is your age. As you grow older, you'll most likely become more conservative in your investing ways, whether its with your personal funds or pension funds such as IRAs, Keoghs, and deferred compensation plans. This evolutionary process holds true for aggressive and conservative investors alike. Figure 1 depicts this.

The younger you are, the more aggressive an investor you can become. You have time to recover and make up for investment mistakes. You can try new investments, ride out the ups and downs of the securities markets, and make major portfolio adjustments every few years. At this stage in life your cash flow is good and discretionary income is high. Should you choose to stash away extra cash for a rainy day or for retirement purposes, you'll have the means to do it.

On the other hand, when you're retired you can't afford to lose big on an investment, especially if you're depending on it to produce income for living expenses. You don't have employment earnings to replenish funds

Figure 1: Age versus Investment Risk

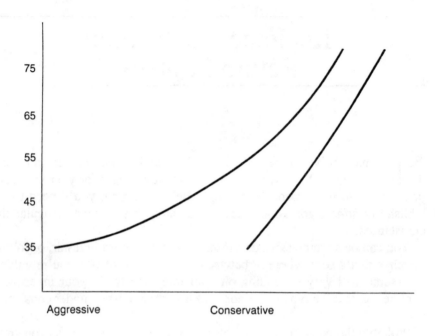

lost from bad investments. Social Security benefits are of little help in this regard. Simply put, at this stage in life it's harder to accumulate any significant savings.

As far as pension and retirement plans are concerned, they should always be invested more conservatively than your personal assets. Most persons will rely on pension assets for a large part of their retirement income needs. Preservation of this capital should be a very important investment objective.

Whatever your stage in life, you want to set investment goals and objectives that are realistic. To the extent possible, the expected returns should be quantified and related to some commonly known financial index as a point of reference. They should also cover a time period of at least several years to allow for interim ups and downs in investment performance.

It's important that you work these goals and objectives out with your investment advisor, stockbroker or other financial counsellor before you set them in concrete. Then everyone, including yourself, is on notice regarding your expectations. Examples of specific total return objectives are:

- Achieve a 12% annual compound growth rate over a 5-year period.
- Beat the inflation rate by an average of 4% over a 3-year period.
- Outpace the S&P 500 Stock Index by at least 3% on average each year over a 5-year period.

By setting forth these objectives, you have something specific with which to compare the total return performance of your portfolio. The greater the risk you're willing to assume, the more demanding your performance objectives should be. For example, if you're going to load your portfolio up with discount straight and convertible bonds, then you should aim for 15% returns instead of 12%. This will compensate you for taking greater risks.

Having developed your goals and objectives, you must decide how to implement the total return strategy outlined in this book. Several approaches may be taken. You can:

- Do it yourself.
- Hire an investment advisor.
- Use the services of a stockbroker.
- Invest in mutual funds.

No matter which way you go, you need to keep on top of your total return investment program through adequate monitoring of performance.

The advantages and disadvantages of each implementation route are summarized in Table 1 below. Notice none of the approaches has perfect scores across the board—"lows" in the own time spent and costs areas and "highs" in the control and tailoring areas. Tradeoffs must be made. In the final analysis, the approach chosen should be the one you're most comfortable with in implementing the total return strategy.

One other thought: You could combine two or more of the approaches. For example, you could manage part of your total return portfolio yourself, and purchase appropriate mutual funds with the balance of your funds. If

Table 1: Cost/Benefit of Total Return Implementation Approaches

	Own Time Spent	Costs of Commissions, Fees, etc.	Control Over Account	Tailored to Own Objectives
Self	High	Low	High	High
Stockbroker	Med.	Med.	High	High
Inv. Advisor	Low	High	Low	Med.
Mutual fund	Low	Med.	Low	Low

your assets were large enough, you could split them between a stockbroker and investment advisor and compare performance. Or you could give your personal funds to one person to manage and retirement funds to another. Either way, you could mimic what many large pension fund administrators do—create a little competitive spirit among persons handling your account. Whoever has the best track record gets a chance to manage all your funds.

Investing On Your Own

Obviously, the "do-it-yourself" total return approach is the most time-consuming. You must come up with your own investment ideas, research them, purchase the most desirable securities, and monitor portfolio performance. Knowing when to sell is an important task. Ideally, you should have a fair amount of investment experience plus a background in accounting and finance. With a flair for investing and through reduced costs, you hope to achieve better returns than the pros.

Plan to spend at least 5 to 10 hours a week handling your account. You probably will have to subscribe to various publications, read others in the public library, and send to companies for annual and quarterly reports. It takes time to read and digest this material. You may need to call company officials to ask about certain matters and get clarification on others. Nevertheless, if you have the talent and time to spend, the "do-it-yourself" approach may work well for you.

If you make your own investment decisions, seriously consider using a discount broker to save 50% or more on commissions. Although you shouldn't be doing a lot of trading, every little bit of reduction in transactions costs counts, especially when the dollar saved will be earning you that much more in current income and, hopefully, capital appreciation under the total return approach. Instead of paying about 2% commission on each $5,000 purchase or sale, with a discounter you'll end up paying less than 1%.

Several statistical services are available through which you can search for appropriate total return investments. Some are publications, others are computer databases. For the latter, you'll need a personal computer, the appropriate software, and a modem. This allows you to search on all stocks in the database for certain characteristics that interest you as a total return investor. You can set parameters to look for stocks with prices of less than book value, price-earnings ratios of less than 10, or yields higher than 6%. The computer will search the database to come up with a list of all stocks with those characteristics. Then you must follow up on them with more research to find those that are the most attractive total return investments.

The Value Line Investment Survey has printouts of all stocks it follows which show the highest yielding non-utility stocks with their estimated year-ahead dividends per share, and those selling at the largest discount to book value. They even provide a list of 25 stocks selected for performance and income characteristics (translation: total return stocks) in their weekly newsletter. Figure 2 provides an example.

Value Line rates each stock it covers according to expected performance and safety, with a "1" being the highest ranking, and a "4" being the lowest ranking. Notice that most total return stocks on the list are rated fairly high (but not highest) for performance and medium to high for safety. They also have yields that are higher than market averages (stock market yields were about 3% when Figure 2 was assembled). Their betas of less than one indicate less volatility than the market. All these characteristics are typical of total return stocks.

Thousands of investors, including professionals who invest for a living, subscribe to Value Line and have access to this same information. Others read it at the local library. There are no secrets in the financial world when widely disseminated research is readily available to everyone. This is the efficient market at work. Only time will tell if Value Line's selected stocks perform as projected.

Figure 2

page 372 VALUE LINE *Selection & Opinion* November 6, 1987

Selected Investments

SELECTED STOCKS FOR PERFORMANCE

Page No.	Name	Recent Price	Rank for Perf.	Rank for Safety	Beta	% Yield	Ind. Rank
1220	Alcan Aluminum ■	22	1	3	1.20	2.9	1
1080	Amdahl Corp.	23	1	3	1.40	0.9	15
1504	Arden Group 'A'	34	1	4	.65	Nil	19
1753	Brunswick Corp.	14	1	3	1.25	2.7	20
276	Burnham Service	15	1	3	.80	1.8	81
2058	CUC Int'l	11	1	4	1.20	Nil	32
1775	Circus Circus Enterpr.	19	1	3	1.05	Nil	52
1086	Compaq Computer	44	1	4	1.55	Nil	15
1317	FMC	31	1	3	.95	Nil	24
351	FlightSafety	26	1	3	1.10	1.0	7
1318	GATX Corp.	34	1	4	.80	4.4	24
790	Genovese Drug 'A'	9⅝	1	3	.70	1.8	51
1513	G't Atlantic & Pacific	32	1	3	1.10	1.6	19
597	Illinois Tool Works	26	1	3	1.00	1.7	8
1321	Kaydon Corp.	16	1	3	.85	0.9	24
281	Laidlaw Transp. 'B'	11	1	3	1.05	1.3	81
2120	Lotus Development	20	1	3	1.40	Nil	6
612	Lukens Inc.	30	1	3	.95	2.3	29
1104	NCR Corp.	55	1	2	1.30	1.8	15
1325	Nordson Corp.	25	1	3	.70	2.0	24
602	Precision Castparts	24	1	3	1.05	0.4	8
525	Raychem Corp.	33	1	3	1.15	0.7	17
1239	Reynolds Metals	30	1	3	1.15	2.0	1
1334	Stewart & Stevenson ■	13	1	4	.90	Nil	24
1522	Weis Markets	29	1	1	.80	1.5	19

■ **Newly added this week.**

SELECTED STOCKS FOR PERFORMANCE AND INCOME

Page No.	Name	Recent Price	Rank for Perf.	Rank for Safety	Beta	% Yield	Ind. Rank
2128	ASA Ltd.	44	2	3	.70	6.8	—
854	Amer. Standard	36	2	3	1.15	5.0	70
1154	Boston Bancorp	14	2	3	1.05	4.3	89
407	British Petroleum PLC	53	2	3	.80	5.3	69
797	Cross (A.T.) 'A'	24	1	2	.85	3.8	82
150	Eastman Kodak	53	2	1	.85	3.5	68
1009	Federal Signal ■	16	2	2	.85	5.0	36
135	Goodyear Tire	42	1	3	1.15	4.0	5
830	Imperial Chem.	70	2	2	.90	3.4	13
599	Kennametal Inc.	21	1	3	1.00	4.8	8
1895	Koppers	32	2	3	1.15	4.1	25
1396	Kysor Ind'l■	14	1	3	.80	3.7	66
437	NOVA Corp.	7¾	2	3	.85	5.1	42
1655	Penney (J.C.)	38	2	2	1.05	4.2	67
339	Philip Morris	86	1	1	1.00	3.9	35
340	RJR Nabisco	50	2	1	1.05	3.8	35
574	Raytheon Co.	67	2	1	1.05	3.0	43
639	St. Paul Cos. ■	44	2	3	1.20	4.0	11
640	Seibels Bruce Group	12	2	3	1.00	6.7	11
1266	SmithKline Beckman	50	2	1	.90	3.5	37
1367	Stone & Webster	56	1	1	.70	4.3	22
2091	Transamerica	29	2	2	1.05	6.3	38
341	UST	23	2	2	.95	5.7	35
1026	Westinghouse Electric	43	2	3	1.30	4.0	36
949	Weyerhaeuser	33	2	3	1.30	4.5	21

■ **Newly added this week.**

Note: One or more investment companies or investment advisory accounts for which Value Line, Inc. acts as investment adviser, and officers, directors or employees of Value Line, Inc may own securities which are reviewed or recommended in this service

Major Insider Transactions†

Purchases

Latest Full-Page Report	Timeliness Rank	Recent Price	Company	Insider, Title	Shares Traded	Date	Price Range	Shares Held(a)
853	1	23	AFG Inds.	D.M. Koll, Dir.	20,000	9/30/87-10/6/87	$31.75-$32.13	30,500
1513	1	32	G't Atlantic & Pacific	H. Haub, Dir.	7,367	9/8/87-9/22/87	$38.75-$39.00	19,960,000*
1175	4	18	HRE Properties	C. Urstadt, Trustee	117,500	9/4/87-9/10/87	$21.00	176,800
1475	—	65	Holly Sugar	W. Grossman, Dir	2,500	8/17/87-9/1/87	$82.00	147,582*
1866	3	4⅞	Rowan Cos.	C.R. Palmer, Chair	405,400	9/10/87-9/23/87	$5.75	N.A.

Sales

Latest Full-Page Report	Timeliness Rank	Recent Price	Company	Insider, Title	Shares Traded	Date	Price Range	Shares Held(a)
1874	5	5⅜	Catalyst Energy	R. MacDonald, Dir.	28,000	9/18/87-9/21/87	$15.63-$16.50	372,000
1279	2	20	Community Psych. Ctrs.	R.L. Green, Chair	63,000	9/21/87-9/29/87	$43.25-$45.38	195,652
1800	2	20	IMS Int'l	T.J. Russell, Chair	30,000	9/15/87	$34.72-$34.75	1,880,800
1480	3	51	Kellogg	T. Knowlton, V.P.	8,000	10/5/87	$63.88	5,000
1802	3	6⅞	Krueger (W.A.)	J.W. Fowler, Chair	70,000	9/8/87-9/24/87	$10.00	322,442
1049	2	27	Molex, Inc.	F.H. Krehbiel, Dir.**	10,000	9/17/87-9/18/87	$51.50-$53.75	2,438,790
1866	3	4⅞	Rowan Co.	C.R. Palmer, Chair	525,410	9/11/87-9/23/87	$9.00-$9.50	12,848
1581	3	20	Service Corp. Int'l	R.L. Waltrip, Chair	76,800	9/2/87-9/16/87	$26.75-$28.75	745,052*
328	2	21	Shoney's, Inc.	A. Schoenbaum, Dir	30,000	8/25/87-9/11/87	$31.75	3,633,373*
1903	—	21	Vista Chemical	C.M. Starks, V.P.	15,000	9/8/87	$45.50-$45.75	26,000

* Includes indirect ownership of common stock
** Beneficial owner of more than 10% of common stock
† Includes only large transactions in U.S.-traded stocks, excludes shares held in the form of limited partnerships, options & family trusts
(a) Beneficial ownership at end of month in which transaction occurred

Factual material is obtained from sources believed to be reliable, but the publisher is not responsible for any errors or omissions contained herein

See accompanying notes to consolidated financial statements.

Source: Value Line Investment Survey.

As far as convertible bonds and preferred stocks are concerned, several services track them and provide data on their terms, conversion premiums, and number of years to breakeven. These are invaluable tools for do-it-yourselfers for picking out undervalued securities. In the alternative, you may want to use the technique of selecting an attractive company first, and then looking to see if it has a convertible security available at a reasonable price.

In order to find suitable discount bonds, the best place to begin is with fallen angel or small capitalization growth companies. For those that look interesting, check to see whether or not they have any publicly-traded issues of straight debt or convertible securities which sell at a discount to par value. You'll find prices of bonds selling on the stock exchanges listed in the financial pages of the newspapers, but the majority trade in the over-the-counter market. Therefore, you may need to subscribe to a quote service in order to follow price movements. Or you can periodically check prices with your broker.

If you're investing on your own, then you'd better be prepared to monitor your portfolio. You'll need to do this quite regularly, but the frequency will be a function of the risk level of your total return account. The more aggressive your holdings, the more intensive the monitoring, particularly of those securities of financially-weak companies.

If the price of a portfolio security starts to drop and you don't know why, call the company and ask to speak to the chief financial officer. Often he has an explanation. Whether the answer is accurate or not may be another question, but you may be able to elicit some valuable information to help you with your hold or sell decision. (Based on what you hear, you may actually want to buy additional shares to average down your purchase price.)

When managing your own total return portfolio, you can set target prices on the appreciation component of each security. When any one of them reaches its pre-designated price objective, sell it and realize your gains. Or in the case of a low price-earnings ratio stock, you might sell it when it trades at the market multiple. These techniques force you to sell in a dispassionate way, minimizing any emotional attachments you might have to a particular security.

Some investors place stop-loss orders on more speculative securities to cut losses in the event an investment mistake was made. You establish a below-market price with the brokerage firm. If the security price drops down to it, the stop-loss order becomes a market order and the security is sold. This protects against large losses, assuming that when the sell signal comes you can get out in time at a reasonable price. If the security price goes up, the stop-loss allows your profits to run, for you're only sold out if the price drops.

A good yardstick might be to sell if the stock or bond price drops 15% from the highest price reached after you bought it. In other words, if you purchased a stock for $20 a share and it went to $22, then started to tail off, you'd be sold out at $18.70 (85% of $22). The problem with this approach is that if the stock keeps rising, you have to continually adjust upwards the stop-loss order price to maintain the 15% spread. But this should be a pleasant undertaking.

Using an Investment Advisor

If you don't want to be bothered with handling portfolio investment and monitoring chores yourself, then you might want to consider hiring an investment advisor. Normally, this person will be involved in the day-to-day supervision of your individual portfolio with discretion to buy and sell securities without having to check with you first. Or you may give him limited discretion, requiring that he touch base with you before making any transaction.

Investment advisors pretty much buy the same securities for all clients who have similar investment objectives. In fact they can save on commissions by purchasing thousands of shares at a time and splitting them among several accounts. Your investment advisor should be able to obtain discounts on commissions from the brokers he uses. The larger ones have been able to negotiate rates down to a nickel a share, even with full-service firms. If yours won't negotiate, look elsewhere.

The main problem with going the investment advisor route is picking the right firm and the right individual at that firm to handle your account. That not only means locating an advisor with a good track record, but one who practices the total return investment philosophy, has the right chemistry with you, and will provide personal attention to your situation. You may interview many persons before you hit on the right one.

The advantage of hiring an investment advisor, in addition to having professional advice at your service, is that his compensation is based solely on the amount of assets in your account. He does not get paid commissions, so there's no incentive to churn assets with lots of trading. The advisor receives a fixed percentage fee. If the assets grow, he'll be entitled to more money; if they diminish, his fee income drops. Therefore, his financial incentive matches up with your goal—asset growth. Except in special circumstances, he cannot base his fee on a percent of profits made in your account.

The annual fee is usually prorated for the time the assets were actually under management. The fees range from 1% up to 2% based on the size of the account. The larger the account, the smaller the percentage. Most advisory fee schedules are scaled downwards. At the $500,000 account size level and above, you may pay less than 1% for assets under management.

Most investment advisors (also called investment counselors or money managers) only handle large accounts of at least $500,000. They are more profitable for them because big accounts don't take much additional servicing time and computer power to handle than small accounts, and the fees are much larger.

A few advisors will take accounts as low as $5,000. But often these advisors charge minimums that raise the actual percentage rate way above the stated rate. If you're not careful, you could end up paying 5% a year in fees. For example, if the advisor charges 1% with a $200 minimum, then accounts under $20,000 will actually be billed more than 1% (a $10,000 account would pay 2% to meet the minimum).

Qualified investment managers at the lower minimum account size levels may be hard to find. Those willing to take small accounts usually have short track records. Money managers typically start out with modest funds. But as their business grows and investment advisory accounts increase in both size and number, the managers raise their minimums. Since they tend to spend more time with the biggest accounts, you may not get the personal attention on your account if it's small in comparison to others the manager advises.

One thing you have to watch out for is evaluating a prospective investment advisor's performance record. His past record can be misleading. All advisors somehow manage to a good job for any particular period of time. You need to go behind the figures and look at the mathematics used to compile performance data along with the risks taken to achieve them.

The method the investment advisor uses to compute performance is important. Take a manager with two accounts, where one goes up 50% from $10,000 to $15,000 and the other declines by 10% from $100,000 to

$90,000. The average return on these two accounts, taken by adding the percentages together and dividing them by two, is +20%. However, the dollar-weighted average amounts to a -4.5%. Quite a difference. The latter figure is a much more accurate reflection of how all money under management fared—it aggregates similar accounts and considers them as one.

The task of finding an advisor can be quite difficult if you have a small or medium-sized portfolio. Some brokerage houses and financial planners offer an advisor selection service. These investment management consultants review the records of many advisors and profile their investment strategies and philosophies through personal interviews. You hire them in hopes that they will select the right advisors for you. The consultants will also monitor the performance of your advisor and recommend advisor switches if necessary.

But the advisor consultants charge for these services, either in the form of wraparound fees or through the generation of brokerage commissions. It often adds up to higher portfolio management costs. For example, a wrap fee, which includes investment advisory fees and all brokerage costs can amount to 3% of assets under management. This is 33% to 50% more than the standard 1% fee plus commissions, assuming low portfolio turnover. The primary advantage of this approach is that you, the client, know what professional management will cost in advance, regardless of how much trading is done in the account.

If you want to locate an advisor on your own, you can contact your accountant or lawyer for local recommendations or look in the yellow pages for help. If you have a pension plan, your actuary or pension plan administrator may be able to help. An outfit called Computer Directions Advisors also keeps track of performance figures for investment advisors, but this is an expensive service to purchase.

At a minimum, expect to receive quarterly performance reports from your advisor. As you review the reports, watch for portfolio turnover and yields. The former should be low and the latter relatively high compared with the market.

Your advisor should be easily accessible by telephone. Request an annual meeting with him to review results and the rationale for chosing current holdings. He should be able to explain how each security relates to your total return portfolio.

No investment advisor should be short-term oriented if he's practicing the total return philosophy. And neither should you, the client, be short-term performance minded. Allow at least several years for the advisor to work his magic. Smart ones ask that they be judged for a minimum three-year period. Remember, it's costly to switch advisors, because a new one will invariably want to sell your old holdings and put his new team of stocks and bonds in place.

Using a Stockbroker

Very few stockbrokers are tuned in to the total return concept. There's no incentive for them to advocate a buy and hold investment philosophy for their customers. Brokers earn their living by generating commissions. In addition, they have no reason to spend a lot of time monitoring the performance of your portfolio. When a new investment idea comes along, they'll look at your holdings, advise you to sell a laggard and buy the latest recommendation. This way your broker earns two commissions.

Some stockbrokers specialize in contrarian investing by recommending high-yielding, out-of-favor securities or discount bonds for their clients. These brokers are worth searching out. You'll be lucky to find one, for they're not in the investment mainstream and probably aren't using their brokerage firm's research reports but do their own research. If you locate one, be sure he has a consistent total return philosophy throughout the investment spectrum.

In searching for an appropriate total return broker, ask friends for help or talk to your banker, accountant or attorney. As a last resort, call the branch managers at several brokerage firms and ask them if they have any brokers in their office who follow the total return approach. If they don't know what you're talking about, hang up the phone and try someone else. Total return advocates may be hard to locate, but don't give up. Who knows, maybe you can train one to use the strategy!

If your account is large enough, you can negotiate discount commissions with your broker. Brokers aren't going to volunteer this information, but at some firms 50% of the commissions are discounted. Your ability to negotiate depends on how much business you give the broker—big accounts with frequent trading activity receive most of the discounts. Unfortunately, this is not a feature of total return investing, so don't expect to be treated like a preferred customer with full-service brokerage firms.

Brokers are faced with increasing pressures from their employers to produce commissions. A successful broker (a big producer, that is) will call you with investment ideas. Because he will presumably be aware of your leanings toward the total return concept, he should only telephone when one of these profit opportunities might sound attractive—you don't want him wasting your precious time on other matters.

As is the case with investment advisors, insist on frequent meetings with your broker to review your portfolio. Ideally, you should get statements that compute the total returns earned to date on each security. Many brokerage houses are upgrading their client reports to make them more sophisticated, yet easier for analysis. They show percents of holdings by industry, quality ratings, current returns, unrealized capital appreciation and depreciation percentages and market average comparisons, as well as other information that makes portfolio reviews easier for both you and the broker.

Using Total Return Mutual Funds

Mutual funds are an alternative to investing total return portfolio funds directly in individual stocks and bonds. They provide a measure of diversification and professional money management not available to the small or average-sized account. Several categories of mutual funds fill the bill as total return vehicles.

The main disadvantages of using mutual funds are that there's no personal touch, portfolios can't be tailored to your special preference and needs, and it's often difficult to obtain a current picture of the mutual fund's holdings. This last is useful in determining the type of companies and industries they like to own. For some reason, mutual fund managements are reluctant to divulge the securities in their portfolios except when required by the SEC every six months.

A $10,000 investment kitty would allow for the purchase of only a few individual stocks and bonds, and not give enough portfolio diversification for most persons. In addition, acquiring very small quantites of securities (i.e., odd lot purchases of less than 100 shares) increases transaction costs. High commissions and markups reduce total returns.

If you want to receive the benefits from a diversified group of high-yield bonds or convertible bonds for your total return portfolio, this might be achieved most easily by purchasing a mutual fund that specialized in these types of bonds. You could buy into a mutual fund portfolio for as little as $500, whereas often the minimum purchase price for an individual bond is $1,000 (less of course for a discount bond). And like small purchases of stocks, the commissions and markups on single bonds can be relatively high.

The mutual fund advantages of diversification, professional management, and low portfolio transaction costs come at a price. The management fee is usually .75% of mutual fund assets. This, plus other shareholder and administrative costs of running the fund, can bring annual expenses to well over 1% of assets. Also, be careful of what are known as 12b(1) fees, which are extra fees some funds charge to cover marketing expenses.

Most of the brokerage houses sell their own private label mutual funds and advertise them as "no-load" funds. But they hit you with a redemption fee when you sell. This starts at 5% for funds held for one year or less, and scales down to 1% during the fifth year and zero thereafter. If the fund performs poorly and you decide to sell after a short period of ownership, you'll be stuck with the redemption fee. This hurts total returns.

The more appropriate mutual funds for total return investors are those pure, unadulterated no-loads funds which are oriented toward the production of current income and have a chance of realizing capital appreciation for their shareholder. Fortunately, growth-income funds, income funds and convertible securities funds meet these objectives.

Growth-Income Funds

Growth-income funds attempt to give investors a reasonable total return based on a combination of long-term capital appreciation and current income. The emphasis is on the phrase "long-term." Most of their portfolios are in stocks which have higher than average yields compared to the holdings of other types of mutual funds. This provides relative stability for an equity investment.

Although growth-income funds may be sluggish while the stock market is rising, their net asset values are not likely to drop as fast when the market is falling. This was illustrated during the market slide which occurred between December, 1980 and August, 1982. Growth-income funds dropped only 10%, compared to 16.5% for the S&P 500.

Several contrarian mutual funds fall into this growth-income category. They invest in out-of-favor stocks loved by no one. When the stocks become more popular and rise in value, the funds sell them. The proceeds are used to invest in other depressed issues. In order to be profitable, the contrarian investment philosophy requires that fund advisors have strength of conviction, coupled with a pinch of patience, while in possession of their unloved, overlooked, misunderstood, and forgotten securities.

Income Funds

Income funds, on the other hand, invest about half their assets in dividend-paying stocks and the balance in convertible or straight-debt securities and preferred stocks. Some specialize in high-yielding common stocks and convertible bonds, and are known as equity-income funds. The fund managers try to generate as much income as possible consistent with taking reasonable risks, but also have a secondary objective of capital appreciation.

These funds perform comparatively well in declining markets. In the September-November, 1987 period, when the S & P 500 Stock Index dropped by 30.2%, no-load income funds declined, on average, by only 16.7%.

Income funds vary widely in portfolio composition. You must look carefully at the prospectus and latest list of fund holdings to determine exactly what you're investing in and how close the fund advisors are adhering to the total return concept. If too large a percentage is invested in straight debt securities, the income fund under consideration may not fit the bill as a total return fund.

High-Yield Bond Funds

High-yield bond funds have become popular of late thanks to the proliferation of "junk" bonds. These mutual funds purchase bonds issued by companies in cyclical industries with heavy debt burdens or by small unseasoned companies. Thus the name "junk." Almost 50 high-yield or aggressive bond funds exist, and each has about 75 to 150 issues in its portfolio, providing excellent diversification for shareholders. The bonds average between 20 and 30 years to maturity and often sell at discounts to par value.

As explained in Chapter 5 on corporate bonds, junk bonds are rated "B" and lower by Moody's and Standard & Poor services. They provide yields from 3% to 5% above current returns available from "AAA," or the highest quality-rated bond. The extra yield compensates investors for additional risk associated with these investments. The yield spread usually widens during recessions and narrows in boom times when the perception is that lower-rated bonds are less likely to default.

The idea behind high-yield bond funds is that through adequate diversification, business risks can be spread among a variety of low-grade issuers. If one happens to default, it will only have a small impact on total portfolio values. Meanwhile, junk bond fund investors are receiving premium yields for not that much additional total portfolio risk. However, absent a drop in interest rate levels, the opportunity for capital appreciation from these funds is low because only a few of their holdings will probably have significant improvements in credit quality.

Convertible Funds

One other specialty fund that should be seriously considered for total return accounts is the convertible fund. These funds invest in a diversified group of convertible bonds and preferred stocks, and have the potential for generating relatively high current income and a modicum of capital appreciation. The concept of the convertible security is fully discussed in Chapter 6 on these hybrid securities.

Dual-Purpose Funds

The dual-purpose fund is an interesting type of closed-end fund for possible total return investment. They were popular back in the late 1960s. Dual-purpose funds are divided into two classes of shares, a preferred stock (also referred to as an income share) that receives all the dividend income from the fund's portfolio, and a common stock (also referred to as a capital share) which is entitled to all of the capital gain when funds are liquidated at some future date.

The income shares are especially attractive for total return investors because of their relatively high current yields and the potential for growth in those yields over time as the dividend income of the stock holdings increases. The high yields make the share prices less volatile, but there's still potential for modest capital gains if the income share price responds positively to growing dividends.

Mutual Fund Selection

Selecting the best mutual fund within the category of funds that is appropriate for your total return needs is not an easy task. You can either consult with your financial advisor for funds that meet your investment objectives, or you can try to pick them yourself. Several statistical services review fund performance and recommend the best funds. Also, Barron's magazine publishes data on mutual funds every quarter.

The most obvious item to check before buying a mutual fund is its past performance. Look at the record for a period of five to ten years or even longer. The key point is to compare each year's total returns to other funds in its group and the market averages. This will give you some idea of consistency of performance, as well as a a good reading on the fund's returns in both up and down markets. After reviewing past history, examine the most recent performance figures, preferably from one to three years out. If both short-term and long-term records look good, then you may have a winner.

Also check to see how long current management has been with the fund. Maybe the good results were due to a hot-shot analyst who has since left for greener pastures. If you really want to conduct a sophisticated analysis of mutual funds, look at the risk-adjusted return (often described by the Greek word *alpha*) and the volatility of the fund over time (known as the fund's *beta*). This is particularly valuable information to have when selecting stock funds. Several services, including Computer Directions Advisors, Inc. and Lipper Analytical Services, calculate these figures for mutual funds. Your broker or financial advisor should be able to obtain this data for the funds you're interested in buying.

Also be wary of large capitalization mutual funds—those with over $500 million in assets. The larger a fund, the harder it is for the manager to move in and out of individual securities without upsetting the market. In addition, the advisor of larger funds may have a more difficult time finding an adequate number of excellent investment opportunities. The breadth of security ownership tends to dilute performance. Often a small fund establishes a superior track record and many new investors rush to join the shareholder ranks. The fund consequently becomes so big that its maneuverability is constrained and performance suffers.

One other admonition: stay away from new funds, unless the managers have an established track record with another fund or advisory firm that's way above average. Often new funds try to capitalize on a stock market fad that's just about to burn out when the fund gets started. Mutual fund investors jump on the bandwagon, only to be disappointed later with poor performance. The follow-the-herd syndrome is contrary to total return thinking.

The final chapter will put everything learned about total return investing into perspective by reviewing how a few everyday, ordinary people—like you—manage their investment portfolios the total return way.

Chapter 10

Building a Total Return Portfolio

Constructing a total return portfolio is no different than developing any other investment portfolio. You build a pyramid by starting with a solid foundation and adding layers until you reach the top. The more conservative investments appear at the bottom and the more speculative ones at the pinnacle. A typical portfolio might look like Figure 1.

Typical Investment Portfolio

At the base of the investment pyramid are holdings of relatively riskless money market funds, short-term bonds, and CDs. At the top are riskier, small capitalization stocks traded in the over-the-counter market, as well as venture capital-type investments in new issues or start-up companies. In between are the blue chip stocks and medium and long-term bonds. Conservative investors never reach for the peak of this pyramid; they will only get to the blue chip stock area. Aggressive investors, on the other hand, construct portfolios that emphasize holdings at the pinnacle.

The total return pyramid is built in the same general way, with conservative holdings at the bottom and more aggressive holdings at the top. Figure 2 is a schematic diagram for a portfolio of total return securities.

Located at the base of the pyramid are the relatively safe, good quality convertible bonds; higher-yielding conservative stocks; REITs; and unleveraged limited partnerships. In the middle are the discount corporate bonds, growth stocks, and the fallen angel stocks. Positioned at the top are low-rated bonds and bankrupt securities which have a high degree of risk of default or are already in default. Although these are speculative securities, they have the potential for producing the highest total returns should the issuing companies pull themselves together and recover financially.

163

Figure 1: Typical Investment Portfolio

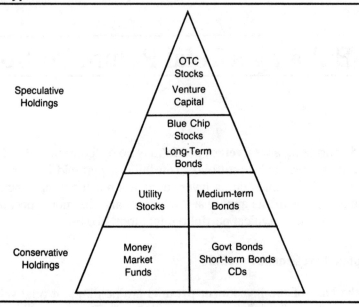

Figure 2: Total Return Investment Portfolio

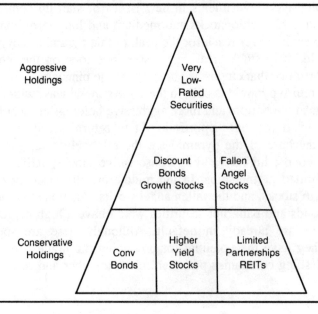

Looked at another way, the securities at the bottom of the total return pyramid provide a large percentage of their returns from current income. As one ascends the pyramid, the proportions change so that at the top the larger part of the total return equation comes from the capital appreciation component. This is shown in Table 1.

Table 1: Origin of Total Returns from Investment Pyramid

	Current Income	Capital Appreciation	Total Return
Bottom third	75%	25%	100%
Middle third	50	50	100
Top third	25	75	100

The percentage of one's portfolio assigned to each category, the composition of the pyramid and the slope of the movement toward the top depend on the total return investor's individual circumstances and tolerance for risk. The number of variations can be almost as great as the population of total return investors.

Each security should play a specific role in the total return portfolio in helping to achieve the investor's objectives. Some are stable and provide high current income; others offer more in the way of capital appreciation. Once that role no longer is valid, for whatever reason, then the security should be removed from the portfolio and a more appropriate replacement found. Total return investing is a dynamic process which requires periodic portfolio adjustments.

The rest of this chapter will be devoted to a description of hypothetical portfolios for a handful of persons in different stages of life, with varying investment goals and objectives. Each is a believer in the total return concept—their portfolios are constructed to reflect this fact. Undoubtedly, you'll be able to identify with one or more of these persons.

Young, Aggressive Risk Minimizer

John Freedom, a swinging single, is in his late twenties and wants to be fairly aggressive with his investment portfolio. He makes $45,000 as a computer salesman and rents an apartment in a condominium in downtown Washington, DC. John has accumulated $25,000 in lifetime savings, which is parked in money market funds and long-term municipal bond funds.

This young man has just read about the total return investing strategy and would like to take $20,000 and try his hand at it. John figures that with lower tax rates for individuals, he doesn't need the tax-free bond income anymore. He'd also like to own securities with more upside potential.

John decides to divide his portfolio into three parts: he'll put the first third in convertible bonds, the second 25% will go into discount corporate bonds and the remaining 50% will be used to purchase some fallen angel stocks. He asks his stockbroker for suggestions. The broker contacts the firm's research department for its latest ideas.

The broker recommends a convertible bond fund because with just $4,000 to $5,000 available for this part of the portfolio, only one or two convertible issues can be bought and high commissions will take their toll. In addition, diversification is needed. The bond fund chosen provides a current yield of 5.5% and appreciation potential of 7% to 8% a year. It has a back-end load, which declines each year John holds the fund.

No bond fund exists which specializes in discount bonds. Therefore, the research department gives John's broker several ideas for discount bonds; the two he picks sell for $700 and $750. John has the broker purchase four bonds each. They mature in 12 years and have coupons of 8% and 8.5%, respectively, and yields to maturity of 13% and 13.5%.

The research department has a list of 10 fallen angel stocks that have good prospects for a turnaround. They carry book values that are higher than their stock prices. John picks five that pay respectable dividends and buys $2,000 of each. Their average dividend yield is 5.5%. According to the research department, if everything goes according to Hoyle, capital appreciation is projected to be 15% for each of the next three years. John's holdings are summarized shown in Table 2.

John's total return portfolio is spread among seven individual securities and one mutual fund. Two-thirds of his expected total return is from the capital appreciation component and one-third is from current income. An overall projected return of 18.3% indicates a fairly aggressive investment stance, which is consistent with John's objecitves. Ideally, he would like more diversification in the portfolio, but if he makes a mistake, he's young enough to recover and try again.

Table 2: Total Return Portfolio of John Freedom

| | Expected Returns (%) | | | Investments | |
	Current	Apprec.	Total	Amount	% Total
Discount bonds	10	10	20	$ 5,800	29
Fallen angel stocks	5	15	20	10,000	50
Convertible bond fund	5	7	12	4,200	21
Total	6.5	11.8	18.3	20,000	100

Conservative, Middle-Age Investor

Harry Jones wants to limit investment risk and is interested in minimizing taxes. He's 45, married, the father of two teenage children and lives in a suburb of New York City. He's an executive with a large airline company in the Big Apple, earning $100,000 a year.

Harry has a $50,000 portfolio that's invested one-third in money market funds, one-third in a corporate bond fund, and one-third in a U.S. government bond fund. Preservation of capital has been a major investment objective of his for a long time.

This successful businessman is becoming more concerned about his high combined Federal and State income tax bracket of 40%. With children headed for college, he would like to build up an education fund in the next few years. Harry is unhappy with the returns from his overly-conservative portfolio. He wants an investment program with more growth potential, yet diversified enough to withstand major financial reverses.

Harry contacts an investment advisor, who suggests he follow the total return approach to investing. Although he's never heard of this strategy, it appeals to him as a way of improving returns without taking on much greater risk. After reviewing Harry's investment goals and tolerance for risk, the advisor recommended the mix of total return securities shown in Table 3.

Table 3: Total Return Portfolio for Harry Jones

| | Expected Returns (%) | | | Investments | |
	Current	Apprec.	Total	Amount	% Total
Discount bonds	12	8	20	$15,000	15
Fallen angel stocks	7	15	22	10,000	10
Growth stocks	5	6	11	10,000	10
Convertible bonds	6	5	11	30,000	30
Real estate inv. trusts	8	4	12	15,000	15
R.E. limited partnerships	7	4	11	20,000	20
Total	7.4	6.2	13.6	100,000	100

The investment advisor contemplates purchasing 20 different securities, and putting $5,000 in each. This will keep commission costs down and allow for adequate portfolio diversification.

This group of total return securities offers a good mix of current income and capital appreciation potential. The real estate portion provides one-third of its current income as a tax-free return of capital to keep Harry's taxes down. This portfolio is well-balanced with 20% in stocks, 35% in real estate and 45% in aggressive bonds. The average current return is over 7%, and the potential appreciation is 6%+. If everything works out, the realized total return will be 13.6%, far above the 8% Harry was earning before he repositioned his assets.

Aggressive, Middle-Age Investor

Joan Carrol, age 36, is married to a small-town doctor in the southwest and has two young children. When she inherited $175,000 from her grandmother's estate several years ago, she quit working to concentrate on raising her children. Joan figured the earnings from the inheritance would replace her lost salary. She gave the funds to her stockbroker and instructed him to be fairly aggressive with them, as she was willing to assume above-average risks.

However, she's not satisfied with the approach her broker has taken with the account. It seems that just about every stock he buys goes up for a while, then something negative happens to the company and the stock drops below the purchase price. Most of these stocks are traded in the over-the-counter market. Even though the stock market has performed very well, her portfolio of $175,000 has not done much of anything.

Through a friend of her husband's, Joan learns of an investment advisory firm in Tuscon, Arizona that employs a different strategy. They buy securities that are out-of-favor at reasonable prices, wait for investor opinion to change when the company's prospects improve, and then sell at a profit. This approach sounds reasonable to Joan, so she contacts them for more information.

At a meeting with the principals of the investment advisory firm, Joan is told in more detail of the contrarian investment strategy, and has a chance to review the firm's long-term record for managing individual accounts. She's impressed with the performance figures and the firm's realistic view of investing.

Joan liquidates her $175,000 brokerage account and sends the proceeds to the investment advisory firm. The funds are subsequently positioned in the manner shown in Table 4, taking into account Joan's willingness to assume a fair amount of risk.

Table 4: Total Return Portfolio for Joan Carrol

| | Expected Returns (%) | | | Investments | |
	Current	Apprec.	Total	Amount	% Total
Discount straight bonds	12	8	20	$ 40,000	20
Fallen angel stocks	5	15	20	100,000	50
Discount convertible bonds	10	10	20	40,000	20
Bankrupt securities	0	25	25	20,000	10
Total	6.9	13.6	20.5	200,000	100

Joan's portfolio is expected to generate relatively high total returns—in excess of 20% a year—if everything goes according to plan. It's about evenly split between stocks and bonds. The advisory firm purchases 20 issues of discount bonds—straight and convertible—and 10 fallen angel stocks. In an effort to boost returns even further, the firm buys 5 issues of bonds and preferred stocks of companies that are either in bankruptcy or have defaulted on their bonds.

Joan's portfolio obviously has risks, but the 35 securities provide adequate diversification to offset the business risks of the individual securities. The biggest potential problem is a deterioration in the economy which would hurt the prospects for these financially weak companies. However, the advisory firm believes it has achieved adequate industry diversification to mollify these risks.

IRA Owner

Mary Malone is a young, single woman in the advertising business in Chicago. At age 32, she's making $45,000 as a junior account executive. She's religiously salted away her IRA contributions since the time they became the universal IRA in 1982. Mary even contributed to her IRA in 1987, although she won't be eligible to deduct the contribution from her adjusted gross income for tax purposes.

She has invested all IRA funds in medium-term bank Certificates of Deposit, and over the years they have grown to $18,000. In the beginning, she earned high interest rates, but these have dropped into the single-digit range. The CDs are about to mature in the next several months. She now feels she has a large enough kitty to try some other investment approach as a "do-it-yourself" investor.

After reading about total return investing in one of the popular financial magazines, Mary decided to switch her IRAs into mutual funds that followed the total return concept. With the proliferation of specialty mutual funds, she felt they could be used to develop a portfolio for total return investing without her having to worry about day to day management of it. Specialty funds invest all their assets either in securities of companies in the same industry or in a particular type of security.

Mary bought a book on no-load mutual fund investing to familiarize herself more thoroughly in the subject matter. She reviewed the records of several funds in categories that interested her and then sent away for prospectuses and the latest performance data on those funds with the best long-term records. As her CDs matured, Mary selected for her IRA portfolio the types of funds shown in Table 5.

Table 5: Total Return Portfolio for Mary Malone

| | Expected Returns (%) | | | Investments | |
	Current	Apprec.	Total	Amount	% Total
Contrarian stock fund	4	7	11	$5,000	28
Utilities stock fund	6	3	9	2,500	14
High-yield bond fund	12	2	14	2,500	14
Convertible bond fund	5	5	10	5,000	28
Real estate fund	7	4	11	3,000	16
Total	6.2	5.0	11.2	18,000	100

Because each fund is with a different mutual fund management company, Mary has to establish five different IRA custodian accounts. She'll end up paying IRA set-up and annual fees on each, but the total cost amounts to only $45 a year. She can sell the mutual funds and move them into money market accounts with telephone switch privileges. All dividends will be automatically reinvested in additional shares, eliminating the problem of what to do with cash build-ups in her accounts. It will also allow her to dollar-cost average new share purchases.

Mary has achieved a good deal of diversification with her selection of mutual funds, although her holdings are somewhat concentrated in interest-sensitive industries, utilities and real estate. Because each fund charges management fees and has other expenses, her returns might not be quite as high had she bought individual securities. This is the tradeoff for less portfolio risk through greater diversification and the use of professsional investment managers. And the relatively high current yield of 6.2%—the weighted average yield on all the funds—compounds tax-free in the IRA, making Mary's retirement kitty build up all the faster.

IRA Rollover for Sophisticated Investor

Jack Savant, age 50, just quit a job with a mid-Western manufacturing company to start a small service company with his brother on the West Coast. He left with a $150,000 pension distribution which was promptly rolled over into his IRA. Including the prior $15,000 in his IRA, he now has a grand total of $165,000 to invest.

Jack has managed his investments all his life. He's been fairly aggressive with his non-pension money, preferring to purchase stocks of small growth companies and speculative over-the-counter securities. Now he's cashing these chips in and putting the proceeds into his new business venture. With the pension money, though, Jack wants to be more conservative. He'll probably need to live off this when he retires in 10 years. Because Jack's not sure how successful his new venture will be, he's not counting on it to provide any pension plan income in retirement.

Jack has just finished reading a book on total return investing. It's the best investment book he's ever read—not just another "how to beat the market" book, but one with a realistic, sensible approach to investing. The concept appeals to him because he feels it's in tune with what he should be doing with his pension money. With the emphasis on current income, he'll benefit from the earnings compounding tax-deferred in his IRA. He also likes the possibilities of capital gains if the right investments are chosen. But above all, he's fascinated with the notion of turning the risk-reward ratio to his advantage.

Jack would like to build his $165,000 IRA kitty up to $400,000 in 10 years without having to add new funds to it. In order to reach this goal, he'll have to earn 9.25% a year on the assets. He feels this is achievable over the long term.

Because Jack follows the stock market and likes to make his own investment decisions, he establishes a IRA rollover account with a discount broker and puts his pension plan distribution into it. He liquidates his current IRA, which is invested in an aggressive no-load growth fund, and adds the proceeds to the rollover IRA. He's now ready to implement a total return strategy with all $165,000.

Jack runs some statistical programs on his computer to select higher-yielding stocks. He follows up with more research on several electric utilities with good growth propects, plus a half-dozen independent telephone companies and water supply companies that appear to have growth potential. Jack picks five convertible bonds with short paybacks because of their low conversion premiums and high yield premiums. He then selects some discount bonds trading on the New York Stock Exchange where the issuing company appears to have good turnaround prospects.

Finally, Jack decides that commercial real estate is a solid bet because it has been depressed of late. The industry looks poised for a turnaround. He purchases the stocks of several real estate investment trusts which employ a small amount of leverage to enhance their growth prospects, as shown in Table 6.

Table 6: Total Return Portfolio for Jack Savant

| | Expected Returns (%) | | | Investment | |
	Current	Apprec.	Total	Amount	% Total
High-yield, moderate growth stocks	7	5	12	$55,000	33.3
Convertible growth bonds	6	8	14	55,000	33.3
Discount bonds	12	6	18	30,000	18.2
REITs	5	7	12	25,000	15.2
Total	7.3	6.5	13.8	165,000	100.0

Jack's IRA portfolio gives him a projected total return approaching 14%. If everything works out as planned, he should easily surpass his goal of building the IRA to $400,000. Remember, all Jack needs is 9.25% a year compounding tax-free in the account. If he were to achieve a 14% compound annual return, the IRA rollover would mushroom to $1.48 million in ten years.

The more conservative portion of Jack's IRA (over 80% of the portfolio) consists of the high-yielding stocks, the convertible bonds and the REITs. The riskiest investments are the discount bonds—but they also have the highest potential total returns. On balance, the portfolio appears quite suitable for someone of his age, prior investment experience, and tolerance for risk. Jack has learned his lessons well from reading the total return investment book.

Retired Person

Paul French just retired from his executive position with a Fortune 100 company and will be receiving a handsome pension as a reward for his 30-year climb up the corporate ladder. He has amassed $250,000 in liquid assets over the years, of which almost $150,000 is in company stock accumulated through the employee stock purchase program. The balance is invested in tax-free bonds and blue chip stocks.

Although he knows his former employer is a blue chip company, he feels the dividend yield on the stock is too low. Besides, he doesn't want all of his eggs invested in one basket after he's left the company. And he doesn't feel quite the same loyalty now that he's not an active employee.

Paul is a conservative investor by nature, depending on his stockbroker for all investment advice. He feels he should look for more yield from his investments, coupled with some protection against inflation should it heat up again. Besides, with his tax bracket dropping over the next several years, Paul doesn't need tax-exempt income as much as he did when earning a large salary.

This former corporate executive feels his pension will be more than adequate to take care of both his and his wife's needs during retirement. He views his liquid investment assets as insurance against a major financial catastrophy as well as comprising the bulk of their estate to pass on to the two children.

Paul approaches his stockbroker and asks what to do now that his life situation is changed. They agree to sell all but $10,000 worth of shares of his former employer's stock. The broker suggests making investments that offer relatively high current income along with moderate growth prospects. He recommends against putting all of Paul's $250,000 capital in total return securities at this juncture, because he's worried about the prospects for the stock and bond markets after their long run-ups.

The broker suggests investing two-thirds in a conservative mix of total return securities with the balance in a short-term bond fund. This way Paul will have some low-risk investments and if the financial markets weaken, he can use reserves parked in the bond fund to buy more total return securities at lower prices.

The recommended portfolio breaks down into the mix shown in Table 7.

Table 7: Total Return Portfolio for Paul Strodny

| | Expected Returns (%) | | | Percent | |
	Current	Apprec.	Total	Amount	% Total
Short-term bond fund	7	0	7	$65,000	26
Employer common stock	2	5	7	10,000	4
High-yield, low-growth stocks	7	3	10	90,000	36
Convertible income bonds	7	4	11	50,500	20
REITs	8	4	12	35,000	14
Total	7.1	2.8	9.9	250,000	100

In this portfolio, the high-yield stocks and the convertible bonds are more conservative and less growth-oriented than a more aggressive total return portfolio. The stocks are of companies in the electric utilities, telephone, natural gas pipeline, and banking industries. The REITs are unleveraged, offer higher current yields but lower growth prospects, and are relatively less risky than their leveraged brethren.

Overall, the portfolio provides a current yield of a bit more than 7%, and annual growth prospects of slightly less than 3%. This satisfies Paul's objectives of a high current income with a small amount of capital appreciation to protect against loss of purchasing power due to inflation.

The several case studies presented above are representative of the variety of situations investors are faced with given their particular circumstances. No solution will be exactly the same for any two people. Fine-tuning of each portfolio is required to produce optimal results. And, of course, total return investment portfolios must be modified as goals and objectives change over time. That's the challange of staying on top of any successful investment program.

Appendix I:
Present Value of $1

Period	1%	2%	3%	4%	5%	6%	7%	8%	9%	10%
1	.9901	.9804	.9709	.9615	.9524	.9434	.9346	.9259	.9174	.9091
2	.9803	.9612	.9426	.9246	.9070	.8900	.8734	.8573	.8417	.8264
3	.9706	.9423	.9151	.8890	.8638	.8396	.8163	.7938	.7722	.7513
4	.9610	.9238	.8885	.8548	.8227	.7921	.7629	.7350	.7084	.6830
5	.9515	.9057	.8626	.8219	.7835	.7473	.7130	.6806	.6499	.6209
6	.9420	.8880	.8375	.7903	.7462	.7050	.6663	.6302	.5963	.5645
7	.9327	.8706	.8131	.7599	.7107	.6651	.6227	.5835	.5470	.5132
8	.9235	.8535	.7894	.7307	.6768	.6274	.5820	.5403	.5019	.4665
9	.9143	.8368	.7664	.7026	.6446	.5919	.5439	.5002	.4604	.4241
10	.9053	.8203	.7441	.6756	.6139	.5584	.5083	.4632	.4224	.3855
11	.8963	.8043	.7224	.6496	.5847	.5268	.4751	.4289	.3875	.3505
12	.8874	.7885	.7014	.6246	.5568	.4970	.4440	.3971	.3555	.3186
13	.8787	.7730	.6810	.6006	.5303	.4688	.4150	.3677	.3262	.2897
14	.8700	.7579	.6611	.5775	.5051	.4423	.3878	.3405	.2992	.2633
15	.8613	.7430	.6419	.5553	.4810	.4173	.3624	.3152	.2745	.2394

Period	1%	2%	3%	4%	5%	6%	7%	8%	9%	10%
16	.8528	.7284	.6232	.5339	.4581	.3936	.3387	.2919	.2519	.2176
17	.8444	.7142	.6050	.5134	.4363	.3714	.3166	.2703	.2311	.1978
18	.8360	.7002	.5874	.4936	.4155	.3503	.2959	.2502	.2120	.1799
19	.8277	.6864	.5703	.4746	.3957	.3305	.2765	.2317	.1945	.1635
20	.8195	.6730	.5537	.4564	.3769	.3118	.2584	.2145	.1784	.1486
21	.8114	.6598	.5375	.4388	.3589	.2942	.2415	.1987	.1637	.1351
22	.8034	.6468	.5219	.4220	.3418	.2775	.2257	.1839	.1502	.1228
23	.7954	.6342	.5067	.4057	.3256	.2618	.2109	.1703	.1378	.1117
24	.7876	.6217	.4919	.3901	.3101	.2470	.1971	.1577	.1264	.1015
25	.7798	.6095	.4776	.3751	.2953	.2330	.1842	.1460	.1160	.0923
26	.7720	.5976	.4637	.3607	.2812	.2198	.1722	.1352	.1064	.0839
27	.7644	.5859	.4502	.3468	.2678	.2074	.1609	.1252	.0976	.0763
28	.7568	.5744	.4371	.3335	.2551	.1956	.1504	.1159	.0895	.0693
29	.7493	.5631	.4243	.3207	.2429	.1846	.1406	.1073	.0822	.0630
30	.7419	.5521	.4120	.3083	.2314	.1741	.1314	.0994	.0754	.0573
35	.7059	.5000	.3554	.2534	.1813	.1301	.0937	.0676	.0490	.0356
40	.6717	.4529	.3066	.2083	.1420	.0972	.0668	.0460	.0318	.0221
45	.6391	.4102	.2644	.1712	.1113	.0727	.0476	.0313	.0207	.0137
50	.6080	.3715	.2281	.1407	.0872	.0543	.0339	.0213	.0134	.0085
55	.5785	.3365	.1968	.1157	.0683	.0406	.0242	.0145	.0087	.0053

Period	12%	14%	15%	16%	18%	20%	24%	28%	32%	36%
1	.8929	.8772	.8696	.8621	.8475	.8333	.8065	.7813	.7576	.7353
2	.7972	.7695	.7561	.7432	.7182	.6944	.6504	.6104	.5739	.5407
3	.7118	.6750	.6575	.6407	.6086	.5787	.5245	.4768	.4348	.3975
4	.6355	.5921	.5718	.5523	.5158	.4823	.4230	.3725	.3294	.2923
5	.5674	.5194	.4972	.4761	.4371	.4019	.3411	.2910	.2495	.2149
6	.5066	.4556	.4323	.4104	.3704	.3349	.2751	.2274	.1890	.1580
7	.4523	.3996	.3759	.3538	.3139	.2791	.2218	.1776	.1432	.1162
8	.4039	.3506	.3269	.3050	.2660	.2326	.1789	.1388	.1085	.0854
9	.3606	.3075	.2843	.2630	.2255	.1938	.1443	.1084	.0822	.0628
10	.3220	.2697	.2472	.2267	.1911	.1615	.1164	.0847	.0623	.0462
11	.2875	.2366	.2149	.1954	.1619	.1346	.0938	.0662	.0472	.0340
12	.2567	.2076	.1869	.1685	.1372	.1122	.0757	.0517	.0357	.0250
13	.2292	.1821	.1625	.1452	.1163	.0935	.0610	.0404	.0271	.0184
14	.2046	.1597	.1413	.1252	.0985	.0779	.0492	.0316	.0205	.0135
15	.1827	.1401	.1229	.1079	.0835	.0649	.0397	.0247	.0155	.0099

Period	12%	14%	15%	16%	18%	20%	24%	28%	32%	36%
16	.1631	.1229	.1069	.0930	.0708	.0541	.0320	.0193	.0118	.0073
17	.1456	.1078	.0929	.0802	.0600	.0451	.0258	.0150	.0089	.0054
18	.1300	.0946	.0808	.0691	.0508	.0376	.0208	.0118	.0068	.0039
19	.1161	.0829	.0703	.0596	.0431	.0313	.0168	.0092	.0051	.0029
20	.1037	.0728	.0611	.0514	.0365	.0261	.0135	.0072	.0039	.0021
21	.0926	.0638	.0531	.0443	.0309	.0217	.0109	.0056	.0029	.0016
22	.0826	.0560	.0462	.0382	.0262	.0181	.0088	.0044	.0022	.0012
23	.0738	.0491	.0402	.0329	.0222	.0151	.0071	.0034	.0017	.0008
24	.0659	.0431	.0349	.0284	.0188	.0126	.0057	.0027	.0013	.0006
25	.0588	.0378	.0304	.0245	.0160	.0105	.0046	.0021	.0010	.0005
26	.0525	.0331	.0264	.0211	.0135	.0087	.0037	.0016	.0007	.0003
27	.0469	.0291	.0230	.0182	.0115	.0073	.0030	.0013	.0006	.0002
28	.0419	.0255	.0200	.0157	.0097	.0061	.0024	.0010	.0004	.0002
29	.0374	.0224	.0174	.0135	.0082	.0051	.0020	.0008	.0003	.0001
30	.0334	.0196	.0151	.0116	.0070	.0042	.0016	.0006	.0002	.0001
35	.0189	.0102	.0075	.0055	.0030	.0017	.0005	.0002	.0001	*
40	.0107	.0053	.0037	.0026	.0013	.0007	.0002	.0001	*	*
45	.0061	.0027	.0019	.0013	.0006	.0003	.0001	*	*	*
50	.0035	.0014	.0009	.0006	.0003	.0001	*	*	*	*
55	.0020	.0007	.0005	.0003	.0001	*	*	*	*	*

*The factor is zero to four decimal places

Appendix II: Limited Partnerships

Partnership Name	Sponsor	Business
Angeles Income Properties	Angeles/Quinoco Corp. 10301 W. Pico Blvd. Los Angeles, CA 90064 800-421-4373	Real estate
August Properties Fund	August Financial Partners. 3545 Long Beach Blvd. Long Beach, CA 90807 800-821-3320	Real estate
Balcor Current Income Fund	Balcor/American Express 4849 Golf Rd. Skokie, IL 60067 312-677-2900	Real estate
Cable TV Fund	Jones Intercable 9697 East Mineral Avenue Englewood, CO 80112 800-572-6520	Cable TV
Columbia Oil and Gas Income	Columbia Securities Corp. 1 Townsight Plaza Topeka, KS 66603 800-255-3569	Oil and gas

Partnership Name	Sponsor	Business
ConCap Instit. Properties	Consolidated Capital 1900 Powell St. Emeryville, CA 94608 800-227-1870	Real estate
Dain 40 Pension Investors Res.	Dain Bosworth 1820 Dain Tower Minneapolis, MN 55402 612-371-7810	Real estate
Enex Oil and Gas Income Program	Enex Resources Corp. 1 Kingswood Plaza Kingswood, TX 77339 800-231-0444	Oil and gas
Enstar Income Program	Enstar Communications Corp. 6100 Lake Forest Drive Atlanta, GA 30328 800-241-1005	Cable TV
Equitec Real Estate Investors Fund	Equitec Financial Group 7677 Oakport St. Oakland, CA 94614 415-430-9900	Real estate
JMB Income Properties	JMB Realty Corp. 875 N. Michigan Ave. Chicago, IL 60611 800-621-1870	Real estate
Krupp Insured Plus	Krupp Securities Corp. 470 Atlantic Ave. Boston, MA 02210 617-574-8300	Real estate

Partnership Name	Sponsor	Business
Merrico Oil and Gas Income Funds	Merrico Resources Inc. 1000 Energy Center Ardmore, OK 73402 800-654-4597	Oil and gas
Murray Income Properties	Murray Realty Inv. 5520 LBJ Freeway Dallas, TX 75240 214-851-6600	Real estate
NTS Properties	NTS Development Co. 10170 Linn Station Rd. Louisville, KY 40223 502-426-4800	Real estate
Parker and Parsley Income	Parker and Parsley Inc. P.O. Box 3178 Midland, TX 79702 800-831-3332	Oil and gas
Public Storage Properties	Public Storage 990 S. Fair Oaks Ave. Pasedena, CA 91109 800-421-2856	Real estate
R.I.C. Ltd.	Realty Income Corp. 200 W. Grand Ave. Escondido, CA 800-854-1967	Real estate
Shurguard Income Properties	Shurguard Inc. 999 Third Ave. Seattle, WA 98104 206-628-3200	Real estate

Partnership Name	*Sponsor*	*Business*
Southmark/CRCA Healthcare	Southmark Corp. 1601 LBJ Freeway Dallas, TX 75234 800-421-3757	Real estate
T.Rowe Price Realty Income Fund	T.Rowe Price 100 E. Pratt St. Baltimore, MD 800-638-5660	Real estate
USSA Real Estate Income Inv.	USSA Financial Svs. 9800 Fredericksburg Rd. San Antonio, TX 78288 800-531-8181	Real estate
Vanguard Real Estate Fund	Vanguard Group 1300 Morris Drive Wayne, PA 19087 800-662-7447	Real estate

Appendix III: Real Estate Investment Trusts

Trust Name	Exchange	Type
Bank America Realty Investors	NYSE	Equity
California Real Estate Inv. Trust	NYSE	Equity
Copley Properties, Inc.	AMEX	Equity
Countrywide Mortgage Investments	AMEX	Mortgage
Federal Realty Investment Trust	NYSE	Equity
First Union Real Estate Inv. Trust	NYSE	Equity
HRE Properties	NYSE	Equity
Health Care Properties Investors	NYSE	Equity
Health Care REIT, Inc.	AMEX	Equity
Health and Rehabilitation Properties Tr.	NYSE	Equity
Hotel Investors Trust	NYSE	Equity
IRT Property Co.	NYSE	Equity
JMB Realty Trust	OTC-N	Equity
L&N Housing Corp.	NYSE	Mortgage
Meditrust	OTC-N	Equity
MONY Real Estate Investors	NYSE	Mortgage
Mortgage Growth Investors	AMEX	Mortgage
New Plan Realty Trust	NYSE	Equity
One Liberty Properties	AMEX	Mortgage
Pennslyvania Real Estate Inv. Trust	AMEX	Equity
Presidential Realty Corp.	AMEX	Mortgage
Property Trust of America	OTC-N	Equity

Trust Name	Exchange	Type
Real Estate Inv. Tr. of California	OTC-N	Equity
Rockefeller Center Properties, Inc.	NYSE	Equity
Santa Anita Relaty Enterprises, Inc.	NYSE	Equity
Storage Equities, Inc.	NYSE	Equity
Trammel Crow Real Estate Investors	NYSE	Equity
United Dominion Realty Trust	OTC-N	Equity
VMS Hotel Investment Trust	AMEX	Mortgage
Washington Real Estate Inv. Trust	AMEX	Equity
Wedgestone Realty Investors Trust	AMEX	Mortgage
Weingarten Realty, Inc.	NYSE	Equity

OTC-N = NASDAQ

Appendix IV: Master Limited Partnerships

Name	Exchange	Business
Apache Petroleum	NYSE	Oil and gas
Boston Celtics LP	NYSE	Sports
Burger King Investors	NYSE	Restaurants
Devon Resource Inv.	AMEX	Oil and gas
EQK Green Acres	NYSE	Real estate
Energy Develop. Part.	AMEX	Oil and gas
Falcon Cable Systems	AMEX	Cable TV
Forum Retirement Part.	AMEX	Real estate
Freeport McMoran Res	NYSE	Agriculture chemicals
Galaxy Cablevision	AMEX	Cable TV
IP Timberlands	NYSE	Timber
Jones Intercable	AMEX	Cable TV
La Quinta Motor Inns	NYSE	Motels
Lear Petroleum Partners	AMEX	Oil and gas
Mesa LP	NYSE	Oil and gas
Motel 6, LP	NYSE	Motels
NRM Energy Co LP	AMEX	Oil and gas
National Realty	AMEX	Real estate
Newhall Inv. Prop	NYSE	Real estate
Rayonier Timberlands	NYSE	Timber
Samson Energy	AMEX	Oil and gas
Snyder Oil Partners	NYSE	Oil and gas
Southwest Realty	AMEX	Real estate
U.S. Realty Partners	OTC	Real estate

Appendix V: Americus Trust Funds

Name	Listed	Abbreviated Name
American Express	AMEX	A-axp
American Home Products	AMEX	A-ahp
AT&T I	NYSE	A Tr
AT&T II	AMEX	A-att2
Amoco	AMEX	A-an
Atlantic Richfield	AMEX	A-arc
Bristol Myers	AMEX	A-bmy
Chevron	AMEX	A-chv
Coca-Cola	AMEX	A-ko
Dow Chemical	AMEX	A-dow
DuPont	AMEX	A-dd
Exxon	AMEX	A-xon
GTE	AMEX	A-gte
General Electric	AMEX	A-ge
General Motors	AMEX	A-gm
Eastman Kodak	AMEX	A-ek
Ford	AMEX	A-f
Hewlitt-Packard	AMEX	A-hwp
Johnson & Johnson	AMEX	A-jnj
IBM	AMEX	A-ibm
Merck	AMEX	A-mrk
Mobile	AMEX	A-mob
Proctor & Gamble	AMEX	A-pg
Sears	AMEX	A-s
Union Pacific	AMEX	A-unp
Xerox	AMEX	A-xrx

Index